IRENE STRANGE'S
CURIOUS CROCHET CREATURES

AMAZING AMIGURUMI PATTERNS
FOR WONDERFULLY WEIRD ANIMALS

DAVID & CHARLES

www.davidandcharles.com

CONTENTS

INTRODUCTION

For as long as I can remember I have been fascinated by the natural world and all its inhabitants. The sheer diversity of life on our planet is mind-boggling, from the tiniest insect to the enormous ocean mammals. And since you, dear reader and maker, are holding this book full of crochet creatures, I bet you are an animal enthusiast, just like me!

I grew up in a very crafty household in the centre of Moscow. My grandma spun yarn, crocheted and sewed beautiful clothes for us and our dolls; my mum preferred to knit. There were plenty of craft books to look through and projects to try out. We didn't keep any pets, but we made up for it by taking in nature at every opportunity. We dived deep into the ocean with Jacques Cousteau to get a glimpse of the amazing underwater worlds, took hazelnuts to the red squirrels in the park and watched for the arrival of snow finches in the winter – the wild things were everywhere if you knew where to look.

Sometime later, an interest in character design led me to discover crocheted toys, and I've been recreating all sorts of creatures with yarn and hook ever since. I think crochet lends itself particularly well to working in three dimensions; it adds structure, and the smooth finish is pleasing to the eye. Since pretty much anything can be made in crochet, I'm particularly drawn to making more unexpected animals – they really don't get enough time in the spotlight compared to the more conventionally cute beasts.

In this book, you will meet 16 rather unusual creatures. You will create furry tummies, spiky backs, scaly tails and feathery necks. Some will have long dangly legs; some will have swirly tails. However curious and unusual, all the creatures you make will be adorably squishy and huggable.

So let's get crafting and get to know some of our more peculiar neighbours better through crochet.

Irene Strange

HOW TO USE THIS BOOK

The projects in this book are as varied as the critters that inspired them. It is my hope that you will try something new in each construction process and pick up a trick or two along the way to add to your crochet toolkit. The patterns range in complexity from quick beginner makes to more involved projects sure to impress the family.

Throughout the book, you'll be working in the amigurumi style, characterized by a smooth, all-over single crochet texture that is worked in a continuous spiral. When using this technique, adding stitches or taking them away can have a dramatic effect on the shape that is created. The projects build on this base of smooth texture and add different effects, either through combining yarns or through using textured stitches – think spikes, popcorns and feathers. Combining different yarns and embellishments brings out the personality in the strangest things.

Use the patterns in this book to kick-start your own exploration of construction methods, colour combinations and textures!

How to read the patterns

When writing a pattern, I tend to think of the shape in terms of repeats: if a shape increases evenly, the repeats are made up of small sections separated into a (bracket) followed by the number of times these stitches fit into the round. It helps to count the stitches as you work to get into a rhythm – the process can be very relaxing, and before you know it the shape will be complete!

Let's look at a typical start to an amigurumi project:

Make a magic ring by looping the working yarn around the finger twice, work 6sc over the looped yarn, then take the ring off the finger and pull on the yarn tail to close the loop.

Round 1: 6sc in a magic ring. [6]

In the next round work 2sc into each stitch of the round, making 6 increases.

Round 2: Inc 6 times. [12]

In the next round work 2sc into every other stitch of the round.

Round 3: (1sc, inc in next st) 6 times. [18]

The instructions in the (round) brackets are the repeat pattern for this round, so work them the number of times written after the bracket.

The total number of stitches – in the [square] brackets – changes between the rounds. This number tells you how many stitches were added or taken away.

Marking the first stitch of the round with a stitch marker and counting the stitches as you work can help you to keep track of where you are in the pattern. You could also use the starting tail to mark the first stitch by pulling it to the front of the work.

With practice it's easy to read the crochet fabric to spot the single crochets (like little 'v's) or increases (more like 'w's) to find your place. Pretty soon you will be able to read the crochet stitches without any markers at all!

Pattern abbreviations

The following abbreviations have been used in this book:

ch = chain stitch

dc = double crochet

dec = single crochet decrease

hdc = half double crochet

hdc2tog = half double crochet decrease 2 stitches into 1

inc = single crochet increase

inv dec = invisible decrease

inv sc3tog = put hook through front loops of first 2 stitches and under both loops of third stitch, pull 1 loop through, complete as sc.

sc = single crochet

sc3tog = single crochet decrease 3 stitches into 1

slst = slip stitch

st(s) = stitches

tr = treble crochet

Crochet terminology

The patterns are all written using US crochet terms. If you are used to working with UK terms, please note the following differences in stitch names:

US TERM	UK TERM
Single crochet	Double crochet
Half double crochet	Half treble crochet
Double crochet	Treble crochet
Treble crochet	Double treble crochet

TOOLS AND MATERIALS

Yarn

The wonderful thing about amigurumi is that they can be made in any yarn! For the projects in this book, I have used yarn from Paintbox Yarns and Rico Designs, with the odd extra thrown in. At the start of each project you will find a list of the exact yarn used and the number of balls each sample took.

A thicker yarn will produce a bigger toy than the sample and will require more yarn. If your chosen yarn is thinner than the sample the result will be dinkier. When substituting yarns, I always compare the length and weight of the yarn ball to the one listed in the pattern – if in doubt it's best to have an extra ball or you might find yourself playing a game of yarn chicken!

While the samples are made in smooth yarns with texture added in other ways, there are many other fibres to explore – try working with chenille or faux fur as well as plain cotton to get a different result.

HOOKS

Finding the right hook is key to a successful amigurumi project. Luckily there are many options to try out and depending on how you hold it in your hand some will be more comfortable than others. I hold my hook like a pen and always use Clover Soft Touch hooks.

Tension (gauge)

To find out if your hook size is right for your yarn try making a small tension swatch (see Tension swatch). For toys, the aim is to create a dense, but not stiff, fabric with no gaps between stitches for stuffing to show through. If the fabric feels too loose, try switching to a smaller hook. If it's too stiff and getting the hook into the next stitch is a struggle, try going up to the next hook size.

Tension swatch

Round 1: 6sc in a magic ring. [6]

Round 2: Inc in all 6 sts. [12]

Round 3: (1sc, inc in next st) 6 times. [18]

Round 4: (2sc, inc in next st) 6 times. [24]

Fasten off.

I recommend the following hook sizes in order to achieve the same size as the samples:

• DK cotton: 3mm (US C/2 or D/3) hook

• Worsted wool: 3.5mm (US E/4) hook

• 4-ply cotton held double: 3.5mm (US E/4) hook

• DK cotton held together with mohair: 3.5mm (US E/4) hook

Remember, these are just guidelines. The main aim is for you to produce a crochet fabric that you will enjoy working with!

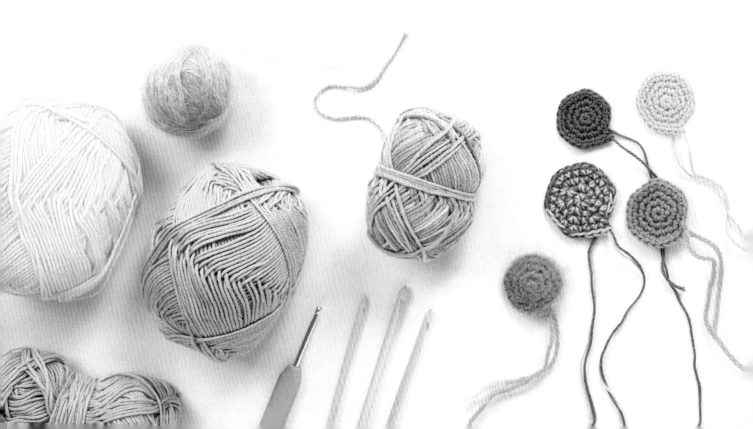

other tools and materials

As well as the yarn and hook you will also need the following items.

TOY SAFETY EYES

Plain black eyes are used for most of the projects in this book, with a size chosen that matches the proportion of each toy. But there are many more unusual, sparkly or realistic toy eyes available online. Embroidered eyes and sewn-on beads also work well; each element you choose will add unique personality to your project. However, if you are giving the toy to a small child, it's best to stick to safety eyes or embroidery.

TOY STUFFING

To give the toys their shape you will need to fill them with toy stuffing. High-loft polyester stuffing is lightweight and versatile; you will find it in your local haberdashery or online. If you prefer sticking to natural fibres, pure wool or recycled cotton stuffing is a good alternative.

FABRIC STABILIZER

For some of the flatter details, a stabilizing insert will help the toy to keep its shape. You can use thick wadding, felt or fabric stabilizer for this – the key is to look for something flexible that bounces back into shape when released.

WIRES

To help the animals hold their poses you can reinforce some parts with wire or craft pipe cleaners (chenille stems). A coated wire, such as 3mm (28-gauge) garden wire, works well for adding a lot of support. Doubling up pipe cleaners adds just enough support to gently adjust the shape.

SEWING PINS AND CLIPS

You will need to have some sewing pins handy when sewing together the different elements of each creature. When joining larger pieces together, sewing clips can work better than pins. Sewing clips can be found in haberdashery shops.

TAPESTRY NEEDLE

For sewing creature parts together, choose a blunt-tipped tapestry needle with a wide eye, so that the yarn is easy to draw through it. The blunt tip will stop the yarn from splitting and protect the fingertips from any prickles!

STITCH MARKERS

Marking the beginning of a round with a stitch marker can be very helpful for keeping on track. You can use a removable stitch marker, a safety pin, a bit of contrasting colour yarn or the yarn tail from the start of the project.

WIRE BRUSH

An ordinary pet hairbrush is the perfect tool for making your crochet creatures extra fluffy!

AARDVARK

Aardvarks sit right at the start of the English dictionary, so it's only fitting that we begin with one! These unusual mammals have remained virtually unchanged for millions of years, making them something of a living fossil. Their powerful feet dig out roomy burrows to hide in from the heat of the sun, long snouts help sniff out the next termite meal and large ears can hear any approaching predator. These nocturnal digging machines are built for keeping armies of ants and termites at bay; they can munch through 50,000 of the wriggly critters every night – quite the appetite!

DIMENSIONS

40cm (15¾in) long

YARNS

Paintbox Yarns Cotton DK (100% cotton) 125m (137yds) per 50g (1¾oz) ball:

- **Beige:** 1 x 50g (1¾oz) ball in Vanilla Cream (shade 408)

- **Brown:** 1 x 50g (1¾oz) ball in Soft Fudge (shade 410)

- **Dark Brown:** 1 x 50g (1¾oz) ball in Coffee Bean (shade 411)

HOOKS

3mm (US C/2 or D/3) hook

Other tools and materials

- Pair 6mm black safety eyes

- Small piece of thick felt or fabric stabilizer

- Toy stuffing

- Sewing pins

- Tapestry needle

FUN FACT

When digging aardvarks can seal their nostrils shut to keep out the dust and ants. Their claws are curved like spoons, which is very handy for all the digging!

Tension (gauge)

Tension is not critical for this project, but if you want to match the pattern shown here, make a small circular swatch using the chosen yarn and hook (see Tools and materials: Tension swatch for the swatch pattern).

When made in DK weight cotton with a 3mm (US C/2 or D/3) hook the swatch should measure 3.5cm (1⅜in) across.

Project notes

The body of the aardvark is worked in one piece starting at the nose and ending at the tail; each section is divided visually with a colour change. The ears and paws are worked separately and sewn on at the end. A small piece of fabric stabilizer is added to help shape the snout.

Special stitches

Front loop only (FLO): Insert the hook under the front loop only (see Crochet techniques: Front loops/back loops).

Ears

Make 2 in **Beige** yarn.

Round 1: 6sc in a magic ring. [6]

Round 2: (inc in next st, 2sc) 2 times. [8]

Round 3: (inc in next st, 3sc) 2 times. [10]

Round 4: (inc in next st, 4sc) 2 times. [12]

Round 5: (inc in next st, 5sc) 2 times. [14]

Round 6: (inc in next st, 6sc) 2 times. [16]

Round 7: (inc in next st, 7sc) 2 times. [18]

Round 8: (inc in next st, 8sc) 2 times. [20]

Round 9: (inc in next st, 9sc) 2 times. [22]

Rounds 10–29: Sc in all 18 sts. [20 rounds]

Fasten off and leave a tail for sewing. **(photo 1)**

Head, body and tail

Make 1, start in **Brown** yarn.

Round 1: 8sc in a magic ring. [8]

Round 2: Inc 8 times. [16]

Round 3: (1sc, inc in next st) 8 times. [24]

Round 4: (2sc, inc in next st) 8 times. [32]

Round 5: (3sc, inc in next st) 8 times. [40]

Round 6: Sc in all 40 sts. [40]

Round 7: Change to **Beige**, work in FLO, sc in all 40 sts. [40] **(photo 2)**

Round 8: In both loops, sc in all 40 sts. [40]

Round 9: (inv dec, 8sc) 4 times. [36]

Round 10: (10sc, inv dec) 3 times. [33]

Round 11: (9sc, inv dec) 3 times. [30]

Round 12: (8sc, inv dec) 3 times. [27]

Round 13: Sc in all 27 sts. [27]

Round 14: (7sc, inv dec) 3 times. [24]

Rounds 15–28: Sc in all 24 sts. [14 rounds]

Round 29: 6sc, (inc in next st, 3sc) 3 times, 6sc. [27]

Round 30: 6sc, (inc in next st, 4sc) 3 times, 6sc. [30]

Round 31: 6sc, (inc in next st, 5sc) 3 times, 6sc. [33]

Round 32: 6sc, (inc in next st, 6sc) 3 times, 6sc. [36]

Round 33: 6sc, (inc in next st, 7sc) 3 times, 6sc. [39]

Round 34: 6sc, (inc in next st, 8sc) 3 times, 6sc. [42]

Round 35: Sc in all 42 sts. [42]

Round 36: 6sc, (inc in next st, 9sc) 3 times, 6sc. [45]

Round 37: Sc in all 45 sts. [45]

Round 38: 6sc, (inc in next st, 10sc) 3 times, 6sc. [48]

Rounds 39–44: Sc in all 48 sts. [6 rounds]

Round 45: 6sc, (10sc, inv dec) 3 times, 6sc. [45]

Round 46: Sc in all 45 sts. [45]

Round 47: Change to **Brown**, 22sc, 3sc in next st, 22sc. [47] **(photo 3)**

Add safety eyes between **Rounds 34 and 35**, checking that the increase from the previous round is in the centre. Cut out a circle of fabric stabilizer to the same size as the snout and place it inside the snout. Add toy stuffing up to the eyes. **(photos 4 and 5)**

The next section is the body, the increases and decreases will shape the spine.

Round 48: 23sc, 3sc in next st, 23sc. [49]

Round 49: 24sc, 3sc in next st, 24sc. [51]

Round 50: 25sc, 3sc in next st, 25sc. [53]

Round 51: 26sc, 3sc in next st, 26sc. [55]

Round 52: Sc in all 55 sts. [55]

Round 53: 27sc, 3sc in next st, 27sc. [57]

Round 54: Sc in all 57 sts. [57]

Round 55: 28sc, 3sc in next st, 28sc. [59]

Round 56: Sc in all 59 sts. [59]

Round 57: 29sc, 3sc in next st, 29sc. [61]

Round 58: Sc in all 61 sts. [61]

Round 59: 30sc, 3sc in next st, 30sc. [63]

Round 60: Sc in all 63 sts. [63]

Round 61: 31sc, 3sc in next st, 31sc. [65]

Round 62: Sc in all 65 sts. [65]

Round 63: 32sc, 3sc in next st, 32sc. [67]

Rounds 64–68: Sc in all 67 sts. [5 rounds]

Round 69: 33sc, inv dec, 1sc, inv dec, 29sc. [65]

Round 70: Sc in all 65 sts. [65]

Round 71: 33sc, inv dec, 1sc, inv dec, 27sc. [63]

Round 72: Sc in all 63 sts. [63]

Round 73: 33sc, inv dec, 1sc, inv dec, 25sc. [61]

Round 74: Sc in all 61 sts. [61]

Round 75: 33sc, inv dec, 1sc, inv dec, 23sc. [59]

Round 76: Sc in all 59 sts. [59]

Round 77: 33sc, inv dec, 1sc, inv dec, 21sc. [57]

Round 78: Sc in all 57 sts. [57]

Round 79: 33sc, inv dec, 1sc, inv dec, 19sc. [55]

Round 80: Sc in all 55 sts. [55]

Round 81: 33sc, inv dec, 1sc, inv dec, 17sc. [53]

Round 82: Sc in all 53 sts. [53]

Round 83: 33sc, inv dec, 1sc, inv dec, 15sc. [51]

Round 84: Sc in all 51 sts. [51]

Round 85: 33sc, inv dec, 1sc, inv dec, 13sc. [49]

Round 86: Sc in all 49 sts. [49]

Round 87: 33sc, inv dec, 1sc, inv dec, 11sc. [47]

Round 88: 32sc, inv dec, 1sc, inv dec, 10sc. [45]

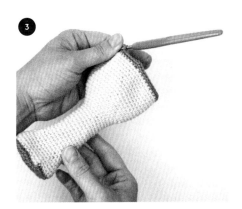

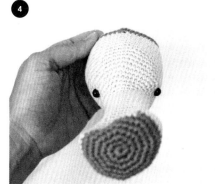

Round 89: 31sc, inv dec, 1sc, inv dec, 9sc. [43]

Round 90: 30sc, inv dec, 1sc, inv dec, 8sc. [41]

Round 91: 29sc, inv dec, 1sc, inv dec, 7sc. [39]

Round 92: 28sc, inv dec, 1sc, inv dec, 6sc. [37] **(photo 6)**

Add toy stuffing; top up the stuffing as you start making the tail.

Round 93: 9sc, change to **Beige**, 18sc, inv dec, 8sc. [36]

Round 94: 27sc, inv dec, 7sc. [35]

Round 95: 26sc, inv dec, 7sc. [34]

Round 96: 26sc, inv dec, 6sc. [33]

Round 97: 25sc, inv dec, 6sc. [32]

Round 98: 25sc, inv dec, 5sc. [31]

Round 99: 24sc, inv dec, 5sc. [30]

Round 100: 24sc, inv dec, 4sc. [29]

Round 101: 23sc, inv dec, 4sc. [28]

Round 102: 23sc, inv dec, 3sc. [27]

Round 103: 22sc, inv dec, 3sc. [26]

Round 104: 22sc, inv dec, 2sc. [25]

Round 105: 21sc, inv dec, 2sc. [24]

Round 106: 21sc, inv dec, 1sc. [23]

Round 107: 20sc, inv dec, 1sc. [22]

Round 108: 20sc, inv dec. [21]

Round 109: 19sc, inv dec. [20]

Round 110: 18sc, inv dec. [19]

Round 111: 17sc, inv dec. [18]

Round 112: 16sc, inv dec. [17]

Round 113: 15sc, inv dec. [16]

Round 114: 14sc, inv dec. [15]

Round 115: 13sc, inv dec. [14]

Round 116: 12sc, inv dec. [13]

Round 117: 11sc, inv dec. [12]

Round 118: 10sc, inv dec. [11]

Round 119: 9sc, inv dec. [10]

Round 120: 8sc, inv dec. [9]

Round 121: 7sc, inv dec. [8]

Round 122: 6sc, inv dec. [7]

Round 123: 5sc, inv dec. [6]

Round 124: Sc in all 6 sts. [6]

Fasten off, leaving a tail. Thread tail through front loops with a tapestry needle and pull tight to close. **(photo 7)**

Feet

Make 4 in **Dark Brown** yarn.

Round 1: 6sc in a magic ring. [6]

Round 2: (1sc, 3sc in next st, 1sc) 2 times. [10]

Round 3: (2sc, 3sc in next st, 2sc) 2 times. [14]

Round 4: 3sc, 3sc in next st, 10sc. [16]

Round 5: 4sc, 3sc in next st, 11sc. [18]

Round 6: 5sc, 3sc in next st, 12sc. [20]

Round 7: 6sc, 3sc in next st, 13sc. [22]

Round 8: 7sc, 3sc in next st, 14sc. [24]

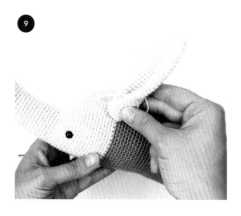

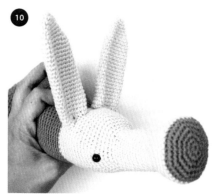

Round 9: 18sc, (inv dec, 1sc) 2 times. [22]

Round 10: 17sc, inv dec, 1sc, inv dec. [20]

Round 11: 17sc, sc3tog. [18]

Rounds 12–13: Sc in all 18 sts. [2 rounds]

Fasten off, leaving a yarn tail for sewing.
(photo 8)

Final details

Sew the ears to the back of the head above the eyes, curving the base of the ears into a U-shape as you sew. **(photos 9 and 10)**

Add some stuffing to the feet and sew them to the body. **(photos 11, 12, 13 and 14)**

Use **Brown** yarn to embroider two lines onto the tip of the snout to finish. **(photos 15 and 16)**

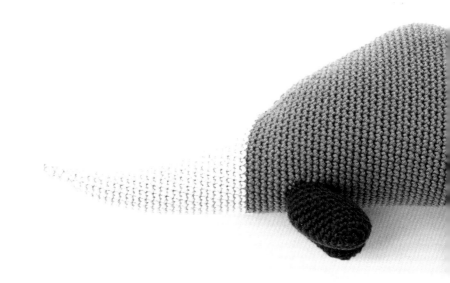

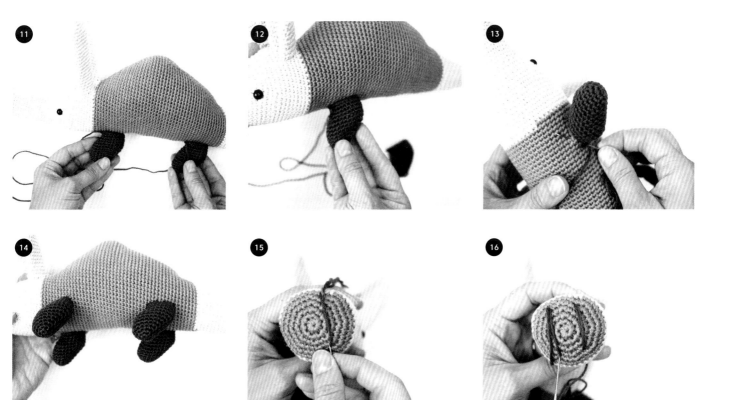

ECHiDNA

I have a bit of a soft spot for all spiky animals, and the echidna is no exception. These charming, slow-moving mammals walk with a delightful waddle, hibernate during the colder months (smart!) and spend their days rummaging around on the ground for ants and insects to eat. They have long, toothless snouts, tiny mouths and extra-long sticky tongues. Unusually, their body temperature is much lower than other mammals, only 32°C (89°F); and, to top it all off, they lay soft leathery eggs – what a unique mix!

DIMENSIONS

20cm (8in) tall

YARNS

Paintbox Yarns Cotton DK (100% cotton) 125m (137yds) per 50g (1¾oz) ball:

- **Light Green** 1 x 50g (1¾oz) ball in Pistachio Green (shade 425)
- **Dark Green** 2 x 50g (1¾oz) balls in Racing Green (shade 428)
- **Pink** 1 x 50g (1¾oz) ball in Blush Pink (shade 454)

HOOKS

3mm (US C/2 or D/3) hook

OTHER TOOLS AND MATERIALS

- Pair 10.5mm black safety eyes
- Toy stuffing
- Sewing pins
- Tapestry needle

FUN FACT

Baby echidnas are called puggles: they are born from an egg, hatch completely spike-less, and stay in mum's pouch for seven weeks.

Tension (gauge)

Tension is not critical for this project, but if you want to match the pattern shown here, make a small circular swatch using the chosen yarn and hook (see Tools and materials: Tension swatch for the swatch pattern).

When made in DK weight cotton with a 3mm (US C/2 or D/3) hook the swatch should measure 3.5cm (1⅜in) across.

Project notes

The head and body of the echidna are made in one piece with paws and claws sewn on top. The spikes are made separately and are worked flat in a contrasting colour yarn, creating a dense texture on alternate rows. The spikes are then stretched over the back and sewn into place.

Special stitches

Front loop only (FLO): Insert the hook under the front loop only (see Crochet techniques: Front loops/back loops).

Back loop only (BLO): Insert the hook under the back loop only (see Crochet techniques: Front loops/back loops).

Snout

Make 1, start in **Dark Green** yarn.

Round 1: 6sc in a magic ring. [6]

Round 2: Sc in all 6 sts. [6]

Rounds 3–5: Change to **Light Green**, sc in all 6 sts. [3 rounds]

Round 6: (1sc, 3sc in next st, 1sc) 2 times. [10]

Fasten off, leaving a tail for sewing. **(photo 1)**

Body

Make 1 in **Light Green** yarn.

Round 1: 6sc in a magic ring. [6]

Round 2: Inc in all 6 sts. [12]

Round 3: (1sc, inc in next st) 6 times. [18]

Round 4: (2sc, inc in next st) 6 times. [24]

Round 5: (3sc, inc in next st) 6 times. [30]

Round 6: (4sc, inc in next st) 6 times. [36]

Round 7: 12sc, (inc in next st, 1sc) 3 times, 12sc, (inc in next st, 1sc) 3 times. [42]

Round 8: 12sc, (2sc, inc in next st) 3 times, 12sc, (2sc, inc in next st) 3 times. [48]

Rounds 9–13: Sc in all 48 sts. [5 rounds]

Next rounds add increases to mark the position of the nose.

Round 14: 6sc, 3sc in next st, 41sc. [50]

Round 15: 7sc, 3sc in next st, 42sc. [52]

Round 16: 8sc, 3sc in next st, 43sc. [54] **(photo 2)**

Round 17: 8sc, FLO 3sc, both loops 7sc (inc in next st, 3sc) 3 times, 12sc (inc in next st, 3sc) 3 times. [60]

Round 18: 18sc, (4sc, inc in next st) 3 times, 12sc, (4sc, inc in next st) 3 times. [66]

Round 19: 6sc, inv dec 3 times, 6sc, (inc in next st, 5sc) 3 times, 12sc, (inc in next st, 5sc) 3 times. [69]

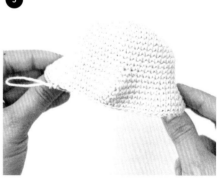

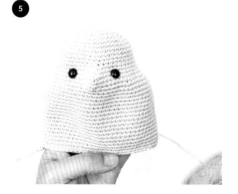

Rounds 20–37: Sc in all 69 sts. [18 rounds] **(photos 3 and 4)**

Add safety eyes on either side of the nose between **Rounds 16 and 17**, approximately 10 stitches apart. **(photo 5)**

Round 38: (inv dec, 21sc) 3 times. [66]

Round 39: (inv dec, 9sc) 6 times. [60]

Round 40: (inv dec, 8sc) 6 times. [54]

Round 41: (inv dec, 7sc) 6 times. [48]

Round 42: (inv dec, 6sc) 6 times. [42]

Round 43: (inv dec, 5sc) 6 times. [36]

Round 44: (inv dec, 4sc) 6 times. [30]

Round 45: (inv dec, 3sc) 6 times. [24]

Round 46: (inv dec, 2sc) 6 times. [18]

Add lots of toy stuffing.

Round 47: (inv dec, 1sc) 6 times. [12]

Round 48: Inv dec 6 times. [6]

Fasten off, leaving a tail. Thread tail through front loops with a tapestry needle and pull tight to close. **(photo 6)**

Paws

Make 4 in **Light Green** yarn.

Round 1: 6sc in a magic ring. [6]

Round 2: Inc in all 6 sts. [12]

Round 3: (1sc, inc in next st) 3 times, 6sc. [15]

Round 4: (2sc, inc in next st) 3 times, 6sc. [18]

Rounds 5–7: Sc in all 18 sts. [3 rounds]

Fasten off, leaving a tail for sewing. **(photo 7)**

Claws

Make 4 in **Light Green** yarn.

Row 1: (ch4, start 2nd ch from hook, work in 3rd loop/back hump, 2slst, 1sc) 4 times. [4 claws]

Fasten off, leaving a tail for sewing. **(photo 8)**

Tongue

Make 1 in **Pink** yarn.

Ch9, start 2nd ch from hook, work in 3rd loop/back hump of the chain.

Row 1: 8slst along the chain. [8]

Fasten off, leaving a tail for sewing. **(photo 9)**

Let's sew the pieces together before starting the back. Pin the paws to the front of the body: the top paws should sit between **Rounds 18 and 22** and the back ones between **Rounds 30 and 34**. Sew them into in place, adding some stuffing into each paw. **(photo 10)**

Now pin the claws to the tip of each paw and stitch in place. **(photo 11)**

Place the snout piece over the nose and sew into place. **(photo 12)**

Then sew the little pink tongue under the snout. **(photo 13)**

It's now time to make the spiky back: this is a little time consuming but the end result will be fab! Alternatively, you could try making the spiky back using loose yarn threads in the same way as cassowary feathers are made (see Bizarre birds & irregular reptiles: Cassowary).

spiky back

Make 1 in **Dark Green** yarn. Work in rows, turning at the end of each row. Spikes are added on every other round.

Ch13, start 2nd ch from hook.

Row 1: 12sc, turn. [12]

Row 2: (ch7, start 2nd ch from hook, 4slst, 2sc, slst in BLO of next st) 12 times, turn. [12 spikes] **(photos 14 and 15)**

Row 3: BLO, ch, (inc in next st, 3sc) 3 times, turn. [15] **(photo 16)**

Row 4: (ch8, start 2nd ch from hook, 5slst, 2sc, slst in BLO of next st) 15 times, turn. [15 spikes]

Row 5: BLO, ch1, (2sc, inc in next st) 5 times, turn. [20]

Row 6: (ch9, start 2nd ch from hook, 6slst, 2sc, slst in BLO of next st) 20 times, turn. [20 spikes]

Row 7: BLO, ch1, (inc in next st, 1sc) 10 times, turn. [30]

Row 8: (ch10, start 2nd ch from hook, 6slst, 3sc, slst in BLO of next 2 sts) 15 times, turn. [15 spikes] **(photo 17)**

Row 9: BLO, ch1, 7sc, 16hdc, 7sc. [30] **(photo 18)**

Row 10: Ch1, (slst in BLO of next st, ch11, start 2nd ch from hook, 7slst, 3sc, slst in BLO of next st) 15 times, turn. [15 spikes]

Row 11: BLO, ch1, 7sc, 16hdc, 7sc. [30]

Row 12: (ch12, start 2nd ch from hook, 8slst, 3sc, slst in BLO of next 2 sts) 15 times, turn. [15 spikes]

Row 13: BLO, ch1, inc in next st, 6sc, 16hdc, 6sc, inc in next, turn. [32]

Row 14: (ch12, start 2nd ch from hook, 8slst, 3sc, slst in BLO of next 2 sts) 16 times, turn. [16 spikes]

Row 15: BLO, ch1, 7sc, 18hdc, 7sc, turn. [32]

Row 16: Ch1, (slst in BLO of next st, ch12, start 2nd ch from hook, 8slst, 3sc, slst in BLO of next st) 16 times, turn. [16 spikes]

Row 17: BLO, ch1, hdc in all 32 sts, turn. [32]

Row 18: (ch12, start 2nd ch from hook, 8slst, 3sc, slst in BLO of next 2 sts) 16 times, turn. [16 spikes]

Row 19: BLO, ch2, dc in all 32 sts, turn. [32]

Row 20: (ch12, start 2nd ch from hook, 8slst, 3sc, slst in BLO of next 2 sts) 16 times, turn. [16 spikes]

Rows 21–36: Repeat **Rows 19 and 20** eight more times. [16 rows] **(photos 19 and 20)**

There should now be 18 rows with spikes on them – don't worry if you end up with extra spikes, the more the better!

Row 37: BLO, ch1, hdc2tog, 28hdc, hdc2tog, turn. [30]

Row 38: (ch10, start 2nd ch from hook, 6slst, 3sc, slst in BLO of next 2 sts) 15 times, turn. [15 spikes]

Row 39: BLO, ch1, dec, 4sc, 18hdc, 4sc, dec. [28]

Row 40: (ch8, start 2nd ch from hook, 5slst, 2sc, slst in BLO of next 2 sts) 14 times, turn. [14 spikes]

Row 41: BLO, ch1, 4sc, dec, 16hdc, inv dec, 4sc. [26]

Row 42: Ch1, slst in BLO of next st, (ch6, start 2nd ch from hook, 4slst, 1sc, slst in BLO of next 2 sts) 12 times, slst in BLO of next st, turn. [12 spikes]

Row 43: (ch6, start 2nd ch from hook, 4slst, 1sc, slst in BLO of next 2 sts) 13 times. [13 spikes]

Fasten off, leaving a long tail for sewing.

Centre the spiky back piece above the eyes and stitch down the top row. **(photo 21)**

Stretch the spikes over the back and down to the bottom, and sew the spiky back in place catching the spaces between the spikes. **(photo 22)**

Then stretch the back piece over the sides of the body and sew in place catching the rows between the spike rows. **(photos 23 and 24)**

Straighten out and arrange the spikes around the body to finish.

WOMBAT

Square heads, square rumps and square paws; these fluffy marsupials may look built for cuddles, but don't get too close – they are armed with sharp claws and can run quickly at any intruder when defending their territory! Wombats are grass-munching digging machines, building elaborate underground burrows to hide from the heat of the sun. Unlike other marsupials, their pouches are backwards facing; I bet that comes in handy for keeping dirt away from the little joeys. But weirdest of all – and most delightful for any toddler – even their poop is square-shaped!

Dimensions

23cm (9in) tall

Yarns

Paintbox Yarns 100% Wool Worsted Superwash (100% wool) 200m (219yds) per 100g (3½oz) ball:

- **Grey:** 1 x 100g (3½oz) ball in Stormy Grey (shade 1204)

Paintbox Yarns Cotton DK (100% cotton) 125m (137yds) per 50g (1¾oz) ball:

- **Dark Grey:** 1 x 50g (1¾oz) ball in Slate Grey (shade 406)
- **Pink:** 1 x 50g (1¾oz) ball in Peach Orange (shade 455) (optional)

Hooks

3.5mm (US E/4) hook

3mm (US C/2 or D/3) hook

Other tools and materials

- Pair 10.5mm black safety eyes
- Wire brush
- Toy stuffing
- Sewing pins
- Tapestry needle

FUN FACT

Wombats can reach unexpected heights with their impressive jumping skills! Some have even been known to jump over 1m (3ft) high fences.

Tension (gauge)

Tension is not critical for this project, but if you want to match the pattern shown here, make a small circular swatch using the chosen yarn and hook (see Tools and materials: Tension swatch for the swatch pattern).

When made in DK weight cotton with a 3mm (US C/2 or D/3) hook the swatch should measure 3.5cm (1⅜in) across. When made in worsted weight wool with 3.5mm (US E/4) hook the swatch should measure 4cm (1⅝in) across.

Project notes

The head and body of the wombat are made in in one piece using a 100 per cent wool yarn and working from the top down with gaps added for the paws. The smaller details are made in cotton yarn and sewn into and onto the body at the end. After assembly the 100 per cent wool yarn is brushed for a fluffy texture.

Head and body

Make 1 in **Grey** yarn with a 3.5mm (US E/4) hook.

Round 1: 6sc in a magic ring. [6]

Round 2: Inc in all 6 sts. [12]

Round 3: (1sc, 3sc in next st, 1sc) 4 times. [20]

Round 4: (2sc, 3sc in next st, 2sc) 4 times. [28]

Round 5: (3sc, 3sc in next st, 3sc) 4 times. [36]

Round 6: (4sc, 3sc in next st, 4sc) 4 times. [44]

Round 7: (5sc, 3sc in next st, 5sc) 4 times. [52]

Round 8: (6sc, 3sc in next st, 6sc) 4 times. [60]

Round 9: (7sc, inc in next st, 7sc) 4 times. [64] **(photo 1)**

Rounds 10–23: Sc in all 64 sts. [14 rounds] **(photo 2)**

The next rounds shape the muzzle.

Round 24: Inc 4 times, 60sc. [68] **(photo 3)**

Round 25: 1sc, 3sc in next st, 4sc, 3sc in next st, 61sc. [72]

Rounds 26–28: Sc in all 72 sts. [3 rounds]

Round 29: 1sc, inv sc3tog, 4sc, inv sc3tog, 61sc. [68]

Round 30: Inv dec, 4sc, inv dec, 60sc. [66]

Add the safety eyes on either side of the muzzle between **Rounds 23 and 24**, about eight stitches apart. **(photo 4)**

Round 31: (9sc, inv dec) 2 times, 22sc, (9sc, inv dec) 2 times. [62]

Round 32: (8sc, inv dec) 2 times, 22sc, (8sc, inv dec) 2 times. [58]

Round 33: (7sc, inv dec) 2 times, 22sc, (7sc, inv dec) 2 times. [54]

Round 34: (6sc, inv dec) 2 times, 22sc, (6sc, inv dec) 2 times. [50]

Round 35: (5sc, inv dec) 2 times, 22sc, (5sc, inv dec) 2 times. [46]

Round 36: 14slst, 28sc, 4slst. [46] **(photos 5 and 6)**

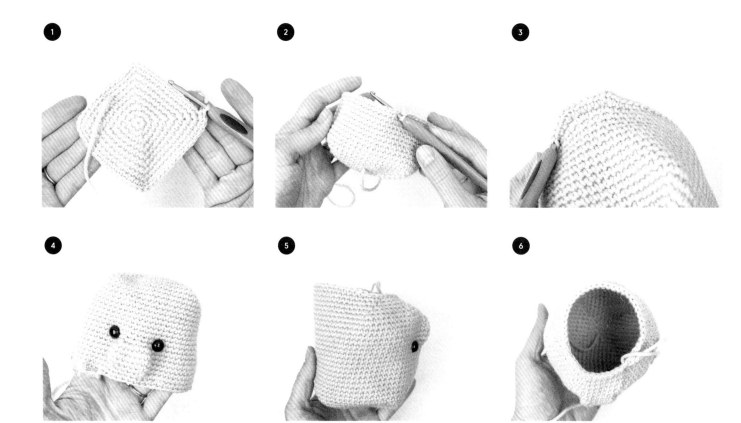

Now let's make the body.

Round 37: 10sc, (inc in next st, 1sc) 6 times, 12sc, (1sc, inc in next st) 6 times. [58]

Round 38: 10sc, (2sc, inc in next st) 6 times, 12sc, (inc in next st, 2sc) 6 times. [70]

Round 39: 10sc, (inc in next st, 5sc) 4 times, 12sc, (5sc, inc in next st) 4 times. [78]

Rounds 40–43: Sc in all 78 sts. [4 rounds]

Next, it's time to skip some stitches to make gaps for the arms.

Round 44: 10sc, ch6, skip 9sts, 50sc, ch6, skip 9sts. [72] **(photo 7)**

Round 45: 10sc, 6sc along the chain (working into the back hump of the chain), 50sc, 6sc along the chain. [72] **(photo 8)**

Rounds 46–54: Sc in all 72 sts. [9 rounds]

Next, it's time to skip some stitches to make gaps for the legs.

Round 55: 12sc, ch9, skip 6sts, 48sc, ch9, skip 6sts. [78] **(photo 9)**

Round 56: 12sc, 9sc along the chain, 48sc, 9sc along the chain. [78]

Rounds 57–58: Sc in all 78 sts. [2 rounds]

Round 59: (11sc, inv dec) 6 times. [72]

Round 60: (10sc, inv dec) 6 times. [66]

Round 61: (9sc, inv dec) 6 times. [60]

Round 62: (8sc, inv dec) 6 times. [54]

Round 63: (7sc, inv dec) 6 times. [48]

Round 64: (4sc, inv dec) 8 times. [40]

Round 65: (3sc, inv dec) 8 times. [32]

Round 66: (2sc, inv dec) 8 times. [24]

Add plenty of toy stuffing to the head, taking care to fill out the nose. Then stuff the body. **(photo 10)**

Round 67: (2sc, inv dec) 6 times. [18]

Round 68: (1sc, inv dec) 6 times. [12]

Round 69: Inv dec 6 times. [6]

Fasten off, leaving a tail. Thread tail through front loops with a tapestry needle and pull tight to close.

Paws

Make 4 in **Grey** yarn with a 3.5mm (US E/4) hook and work around the gaps created in **Rounds 44 and 55**.

Round 1: Join in yarn to any stitch, work 15sc around the gap. [15]

Rounds 2–6: Sc in all 15 sts. [5 rounds]

Round 7: (1sc, inv dec) 5 times. [10]

Fasten off, leaving a tail for sewing the claws in. Add some stuffing to the paws through the gaps. **(photo 11)**

claws

Make 4 in **Dark Grey** yarn with a 3mm (US C/2 or D/3) hook. Work in rows.

Ch6, start 2nd ch from hook.

Row 1: 1sc in each ch, turn. [5]

Row 2: (ch4, work into the back humps of the chain, 2slst, 2sc, slst in next st from Row 1) 4 times. [4 claws]

Fasten off. **(photos 12 and 13)**

ears

Make 2 in **Grey** yarn with a 3.5mm (US E/4) hook

Round 1: 5sc in a magic ring. [5]

Round 2: Inc in all 5 sts. [10]

Round 3: (1sc, inc in next st) 5 times. [15]

Round 4: (2sc, inc in next st) 5 times. [20]

Round 5: (3sc, inc in next st) 5 times. [25]

Round 6: (4sc, inc in next st) 5 times. [30]

Fasten off, leaving a long tail for sewing. **(photo 14)**

nose

Make 1 in **Dark Grey** yarn with a 3mm (US C/2 or D/3) hook

Round 1: 6sc in a magic ring. [6]

Round 2: Inc in all 6 sts. [12]

Round 3: (1sc, 3sc in next st, 1sc) 4 times. [20]

Fasten off, leaving a tail for sewing.

12

13

14

15

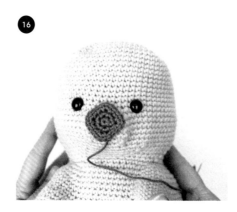

16

17

Final details

Place the claws into the paw openings and sew them shut with the **Grey** yarn tail. **(photo 15)**

Sew the nose to the muzzle, angling it like a diamond shape. **(photo 16)**

Fold the ear pieces flat and sew them to the top of the head between **Rounds 6 and 10**. **(photos 17 and 18)**

Except for the area around the nose, brush out all of the **Grey** yarn with a wire brush. **(photo 19)**

Embroider the mouth underneath the nose using the **Dark Grey** yarn. **(photo 20)**

optional details

I love adding extra details to the toys; however, if you prefer a simpler project, you could stop now as the next few pieces are optional.

PALMS (OPTIONAL)

Make 4 in **Pink** yarn with a 3mm (US C/2 or D/3) hook.

Round 1: 6sc in a magic ring. [6]

Round 2: (1sc, 3sc in next st) 3 times. [12]

Fasten off, leaving a long tail for sewing and embroidery.

Sew the **Pink** palms to each paw. **(photo 21)**

TINY TAIL (OPTIONAL)

If you want to add a tail, make 1 in **Grey** yarn with a 3.5mm (US E/4) hook.

Round 1: 5sc in a magic ring. [5]

Round 2: Inc in all 5 sts. [10]

Round 3: Sc in all 10 sts. [10]

Fasten off, leaving a tail for sewing.

Sew the tiny tail to the back of the wombat. **(photo 22)**

POUCH (OPTIONAL)

If you want to add a pouch, make 1 in **Grey** yarn with a 3.5mm (US E/4) hook.

Round 1: 6sc in a magic ring. [6]

Round 2: Inc in all 6 sts. [12]

Round 3: (1sc, 3sc in next st, 1sc) 4 times. [20]

Round 4: (2sc, 3sc in next st, 2sc) 4 times. [28]

Round 5: (3sc, 3sc in next st, 3sc) 4 times. [36]

Round 6: Sc in all 36 sts. [36]

Fasten off, leaving a long tail for sewing.

Brush out the pouch with the wire brush and sew it onto the lower half of the tummy, leaving an opening along the lower edge. **(photo 23)**

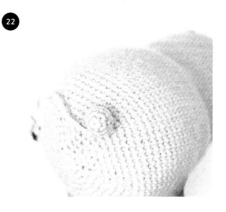

ORANGUTAN

Bright orange fur, big quizzical eyes and awkwardly long limbs – orangutans are our adorable, scruffy cousins! These fascinating mammals spend most of their lives moving through the tree canopy (which is quite a feat considering their large size!) and feasting on fruit. Orangutans are known for their intelligence: just like us, baby orangutans learn many skills by copying their parents. And, just like us, they really are creatures of comfort; I especially love seeing them make leafy umbrellas when it rains and snuggling down in their treetop nests to sleep on leafy pillows. What could be cuter?

Dimensions

48cm (19in) tall

Yarns

Paintbox Yarns 100% Wool Worsted Superwash (100% wool) 200m (219yds) per 100g (3½oz) ball:

- **Warm Orange:** 3 x 100g (3½oz) balls in Vintage Pink (shade 1255)

Paintbox Yarns Cotton DK (100% cotton) 125m (137yds) per 50g (1¾oz) ball:

- **Pale Orange:** 2 x 50g (1¾oz) balls in Peach Orange (shade 455)

Hooks

3.5mm (US E/4) hook

3mm (US C/2 or D/3) hook

Other tools and materials

- Pair 18mm black safety eyes
- Wire brush
- Toy stuffing
- Sewing pins
- Tapestry needle
- Pen

FUN FACT

The orangutan is taller sideways! Its arm span is longer than its height and can reach more than 2m (7ft) from fingertip to fingertip.

Tension (gauge)

Tension is not critical for this project, but if you want to match the pattern shown, make a small circular swatch using the chosen yarn and hook (see Tools and materials: Tension swatch for the swatch pattern).

When made in DK weight cotton with a 3mm (US C/2 or D/3) hook the swatch should measure 3.5cm (1⅜in) across.

When made in worsted weight wool with 3.5mm (US E/4) hook the swatch should measure 4cm (1⅝in) across.

Project notes

The head and body are made in a 100 per cent wool yarn, which is brushed after assembly to create a fluffy texture. The arms and legs are joined to the body by crochet but could be sewn on instead (see Assembly techniques). The facial details, hands and feet are made in cotton yarn, with the muzzle sewn onto the head at the end.

Thumbs and big toes

Make 4 in **Pale Orange** yarn with a 3mm (US C/2 or D/3) hook.

Round 1: 6sc in a magic ring. [6]

Round 2: Inc in all 6 sts. [12]

Rounds 3–9: Sc in all 12 sts. [7 rounds]

Fasten off, set aside. **(photo 1)**

Arms

The arms and legs are worked in the same way, but the legs are shorter.

Make 2, start in **Pale Orange** yarn with a 3mm (US C/2 or D/3) hook.

Round 1: 6sc in a magic ring. [6]

Round 2: (1sc, 3sc in next st, 1sc) 2 times. [10]

Round 3: (2sc, 3sc in next st, 2sc) 2 times. [14]

Round 4: (3sc, 3sc in next st, 3sc) 2 times. [18]

Round 5: (4sc, 3sc in next st, 4sc) 2 times. [22]

Round 6: (5sc, 3sc in next st, 5sc) 2 times. [26]

Round 7: (6sc, 3sc in next st, 6sc) 2 times. [30]

Round 8: (7sc, 3sc in next st, 7sc) 2 times. [34] **(photo 2)**

Rounds 9–18: Sc in all 34 sts. [10 rounds]

In the next round we will join in the thumb.

Round 19: 10sc, bring the thumb in line with the work, 12sc around the thumb, carry on along the main round, 24sc. [46] **(photos 3 and 4)**

Rounds 20–21: Sc in all 46 sts. [2 rounds]

Round 22: 14sc, inv dec 2 times, 28sc. [44]

Round 23: Sc in all 44 sts.

Round 24: 13sc, inv dec 2 times, 27sc. [42]

Round 25: Sc in all 42 sts.

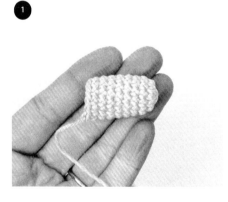

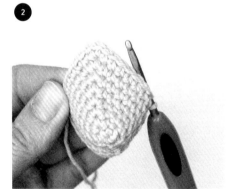

Round 26: 12sc, inv dec 2 times, 26sc. [40]

Round 27: Sc in all 40 sts.

Round 28: (inv dec, 6sc) 5 times. [35]

Round 29: (inv dec, 5sc) 5 times. [30]

Round 30: Sc in all 30 sts.

Round 31: Change to **Warm Orange** and a 3.5mm (US E/4) hook. Sc in all 30 sts. **(photo 5)**

Rounds 32–61: Sc in all 30 sts. [30 rounds]

Round 62: 9sc, (inv dec, 3sc) 3 times, 6sc. [27]

Round 63: 9sc, (inv dec, 2sc) 3 times, 6sc. [24] **(photo 6)**

The next round adds a chain gap in the arm, which will allow you to create the elbow later.

Round 64: 9sc, ch21, skip 9sts, 6sc. [15 + 21ch] **(photos 7 and 8)**

Round 65: 9sc, 21sc along the chain, 6sc. [36] **(photo 9)**

Rounds 66–89: Sc in all 36 sts. [24 rounds]

Round 90: 9sc, (inv dec, 5sc) 3 times, 6sc. [33]

Round 91: 9sc, (inv dec, 4sc) 3 times, 6sc. [30]

Round 92: (inv dec, 3sc) 6 times. [24] **(photo 10)**

Fasten off and add stuffing to the hand and lower arm section and set aside.

Legs

Make 2, start in **Pale Orange** yarn with a 3mm (US C/2 or D/3) hook.

Rounds 1–31: Work in the same way as for the arms.

Rounds 32–51: Sc in all 30 sts. [20 rounds]

Round 52: 8sc, (inv dec, 3sc) 3 times, 7sc. [27]

Round 53: 8sc, (inv dec, 2sc) 3 times, 7sc. [24]

The next round adds a chain gap in the leg, which will allow you to create the knee later.

Round 54: 8sc, ch21, skip 9sts, 7sc. [15 + 21ch]

Round 55: 8sc, 21sc along the chain, 7sc. [36]

Rounds 56–75: Sc in all 36 sts. [20 rounds]

Round 76: 8sc, (inv dec, 5sc) 3 times, 7sc. [33]

Round 77: 8sc, (inv dec, 4sc) 3 times, 7sc. [30]

Round 78: (inv dec, 3sc) 6 times. [24]

Fasten off, add stuffing to the feet and lower leg section and set aside. **(photo 11)**

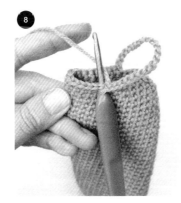

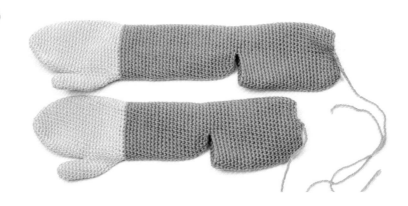

To shape the hands and feet, sew two seams onto them, dividing them into fingers and toes. Use your preferred hand-sewing stitch for this; I like to use back stitch for a strong seam. **(photos 12 and 13)**

BODY

Make 1 in **Warm Orange** yarn with a 3.5mm (US E/4) hook.

Round 1: 7sc in a magic ring. [7]

Round 2: Inc in all 7 sts. [14]

Round 3: (1sc, inc in next st) 7 times. [21]

Round 4: (2sc, inc in next st) 7 times. [28]

Round 5: (3sc, inc in next st) 7 times. [35]

Round 6: (4sc, inc in next st) 7 times. [42]

Rounds 7–8: Sc in all 42 sts. [2 rounds]

Round 9: (6sc, inc in next st) 6 times. [48]

Round 10: Sc in all 48 sts.

The next round joins in the legs. Place the legs onto a work surface with the big toes pointing in. If you'd prefer to sew the legs on at the end you can chain 16 and skip 8 body stitches instead of crocheting through the layers together; this will create gaps in the fabric.

Round 11: 8sc, 8sc along both the body and the lower edge of the leg (the section closest to the work surface), 16sc along body, 8sc along both the body and the lower edge of next leg, taking care the thumbs are pointing inwards, 8sc along the body. [48] **(photo 14)**

Round 12: 8sc, 16sc along the remaining free leg stitches, skip 8 stitches on the joined leg, 16sc along the body, 16sc along the next leg, skip the 8 stitches that join the leg, 8sc along the body. [64] **(photo 15)**

Rounds 13–22: Sc in all 64 sts. [10 rounds]

The next round is where the shaping for the tummy starts.

Round 23: 16sc, (inv dec, 2sc) 8 times, 16sc. [56]

Round 24: 16sc, (1sc, inv dec) 8 times, 16sc. [48]

Rounds 25–34: Sc in all 48 sts. [10 rounds] **(photo 16)**

Now it's time to add in the arms. When attaching the arms, check that the thumbs are pointing to the top of the work and that the elbow folds are the right way up. **(photo 17)** If you'd prefer to sew the arms in at the end, you can ch12 and skip 12 body stitches instead of crocheting the layers together; this will create gaps in the fabric.

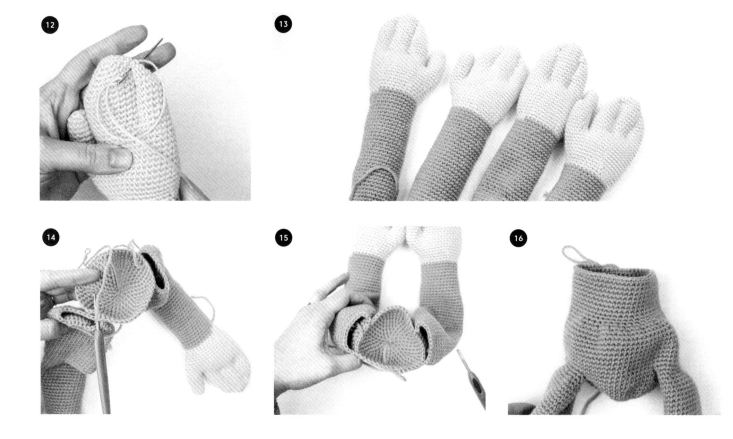

Round 35: 8sc, 12sc along both the layer of arm closest to body and the body, 12sc along the front of body, 12sc along both the closest layer of arm and body, 4sc. [48] **(photo 18)**

Round 36: 8sc, 12sc along the remaining free stitches of the arm, skip 12 body stitches, 12sc along the front of body, 12sc along the next free 12 stitches of the arm, skip 12 body/arm stitches, 4sc along the body. [48] **(photo 19)**

Round 37: Sc in all 48sts.

Round 38: (6sc, inv dec) 6 times. [42]

Round 39: (5sc, inv dec) 6 times. [36]

Round 40: (4sc, inv dec) 6 times. [30]

Round 41: Slst in all 30 sts.

Fasten off, leaving a tail for sewing. Add lots of stuffing to the body.

Head

Make 1 in **Warm Orange** yarn with a 3.5mm (US E/4) hook.

Round 1: 7sc in a magic ring. [7]

Round 2: Inc in all 7 sts. [14]

Round 3: (1sc, inc in next st) 7 times. [21]

Round 4: (2sc, inc in next st) 7 times. [28]

Round 5: (3sc, inc in next st) 7 times. [35]

Round 6: (4sc, inc in next st) 7 times. [42]

Round 7: (6sc, inc in next st) 6 times. [48]

Rounds 8–10: Sc in all 48 sts. [3 rounds]

Round 11: (7sc, inc in next st) 6 times. [54]

Rounds 12–14: Sc in all 54 sts. [3 rounds]

Round 15: (8sc, inc in next st) 6 times. [60]

Rounds 16–25: Sc in all 60 sts. [10 rounds]

Increases for the muzzle start in the next round.

Round 26: 24sc, (inc in next st, 1sc) 6 times, 24sc. [66]

Round 27: 24sc, (2sc, inc in next st) 6 times, 24sc. [72] **(photo 20)**

Round 28–35: Sc in all 72 sts. [8 rounds]

Round 36: (10sc, inv dec) 6 times. [66]

Round 37: (9sc, inv dec) 6 times. [60]

Round 38: (8sc, inv dec) 6 times. [54]

Round 39: (7sc, inv dec) 6 times. [48]

Round 40: (6sc, inv dec) 6 times. [42]

Round 41: (5sc, inv dec) 6 times. [36]

Round 42: (4sc, inv dec) 6 times. [30]

Fasten off.

Add the safety eyes, approximately 7 stitches apart, between **Rounds 22 and 23**, above the muzzle increases. (photo 21)

Add lots of stuffing and sew the head and body together (see Assembly techniques). **(photo 22)**

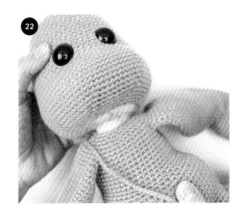

Face patch

Make 1 in **Pale Orange** yarn with a 3mm (US C/2 or D/3) hook.

Round 1: 7sc in a magic ring. [7]

Round 2: Inc in all 7 sts. [14]

Round 3: (1sc, inc in next st) 7 times. [21]

Round 4: (2sc, inc in next st) 7 times. [28]

Round 5: (3sc, inc in next st) 7 times. [35]

Round 6: (4sc, inc in next st) 7 times. [42]

Round 7: (5sc, inc in next st) 7 times. [49]

Round 8: (6sc, inc in next st) 7 times. [56]

Rounds 9–16: Sc in all 56 sts. [6 rounds]

Fasten off, leaving an extra-long tail for sewing.

FINISHING THE FACE PATCH

Turn the face patch wrong side out and draw a line across the middle to mark out the mouth. **(photo 23)**

Sew a seam along this line, creating a fold in the fabric. **(photo 24)**

Turn the face patch right side out and pin it to the front of the head, covering the muzzle increases. **(photo 25)**

Carefully sew the patch in place, adding a bit of stuffing underneath to fill it out. **(photo 26)**

Ears

Make 2 in **Pale Orange** yarn with a 3mm (US C/2 or D/3) hook.

Round 1: 6sc in a magic ring. [6]

Round 2: Inc in all 6 sts. [12]

Round 3: Inc 7 times, 5slst. [19]

Round 4: 14sc, 5sc into the slst. [19]

Round 5: 14sc, slst into next st, skip the remaining sts. [15]

Fasten off, leaving a tail for sewing.

Fold the parts of the ears with the increases to form the ear shape. **(photo 27)** Sew the ears to the side of the head, a little below the eyes. **(photo 28)**

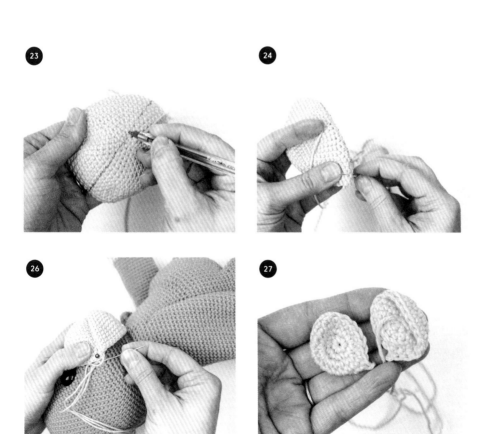

Final Details

Using the hole created by the chain gap, add lots of stuffing to the arms and legs. Fold the arms and legs along the gaps to form the elbows and the knees. Adjust the fold to your liking to make the elbows pointier. Pin and sew up the gaps. **(photo 29)**

Using **Pale Orange** yarn, embroider the nose in the centre of the face patch, positioning it between the eyes. First, make two short stitches over the surface – a small distance apart – then wrap the yarn around those two stitches to build them up. **(photo 30)**

Using the wire brush, brush all of the **Warm Orange** sections to make your orangutan fluffy. Move your brush in different directions to build up a fuzzy layer all over – the more you brush the fabric, the fluffier it will be. **(photo 31)**

To finish, embroider some little wrinkles around the eyes using the **Pale Orange** yarn. **(photo 32)**

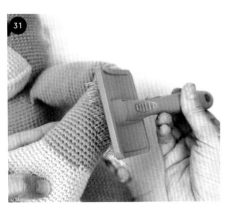

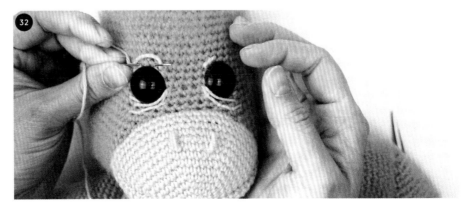

SLENDER LORIS

High up in the tree canopy the slender loris creeps silently along the branches, large eyes wide open to take in the night. Let's pause to admire this perfect nocturnal hunter. These primitive mammals spend their nights alone, foraging for insects, shoots and fruit. Because they don't have a tail, they need a continuous tree canopy to hunt successfully – they can't jump from tree to tree like other primates. And what is the best way to spend the day after a busy night of hunting? Why, high up in the canopy, curled up in a ball, fast asleep next to their friends, of course!

Dimensions

20cm (8in) long

Yarns

Paintbox Yarns Cotton DK (100% cotton), 125m (137yds) per 50g (1¾oz) ball:

- **Brown:** 2 x 50g (1¾oz) balls in Soft Fudge (shade 410)
- **Beige:** 1 x 50g (1¾oz) ball in Light Caramel (shade 409)
- **Dark Brown:** 1 x 50g (1¾oz) ball in Coffee Bean (shade 411)
- **Orange:** 1 x 50g (1¾oz) ball in Melon Sorbet (shade 417)

Lain'amourée Orphée Lace Weight Mohair (72% mohair, 28% silk), 420m (459yds) per 50g (1¾oz) ball:

- **Caramel Mohair:** 1 x 50g (1¾oz) ball in Caramel Au Beurre Salé

Hooks

3mm (US C/2 or D/3) hook

Other tools and materials

- Pair 6mm black safety eyes
- Craft pipe cleaners (chenille stems) or wire (optional)
- Toy stuffing
- Sewing pins
- Tapestry needle

FUN FACT

Lorises have opposable thumbs, just like humans, making it easier for them to grasp onto tree trunks. They are much better climbers than us though!

Tension (gauge)

Tension is not critical for this project, but if you want to match the pattern shown here, make a small circular swatch using the chosen yarn and hook (see Tools and materials: Tension swatch for the swatch pattern).

When made in DK weight cotton with a 3mm (US C/2 or D/3) hook the swatch should measure 3.5cm (1⅜in) across.

Project notes

The body is worked in one piece from the tip of the nose to the bottom. There are gaps in the body for joining in the arms and legs. The eyes are sewn on separately as patches. Adding a strand of mohair into the body yarn creates a lovely, fluffy halo effect to the finished toy. Any lace weight mohair in a complementary colour will work but if you wish, you could replace this with a lace-weight wool or make it in a chenille yarn instead.

Eyes

Make 2 in **Orange** yarn.

Round 1: 6sc in a magic ring. [6]

Round 2: Inc in all 6 sts. [12]

Round 3: (1sc, inc in next st) 6 times. [18]

Round 4: Sc in all 18 sts. [18]

Round 5: Slst in all 18 sts. [18]

Fasten off and weave in the yarn end. **(photo 1)**

Left eye patch

Make 1 in **Dark Brown** yarn.

Join **Dark Brown** to any slip stitch from **Round 5** of the eyes.

Round 1: (2sc, inc in next st) 6 times. [24] **(photo 2)**

Round 2: 3sc, 3sc in next st, 4sc, 4slst, (3sc, inc in next st) 3 times. [29]

Round 3: 4sc, 3sc in next st, 3sc, slst in next st, skip the remaining sts. [11]

Fasten off, leaving a tail for sewing.

Right eye patch

Make 1 in **Dark Brown** yarn.

Join **Dark Brown** to any slip stitch from **Round 5** of the eyes.

Round 1: (2sc, inc in next st) 6 times. [24]

Round 2: 3sc, 3sc in next st, 4slst, (3sc, inc in next st) 4 times. [30]

Round 3: 4sc, 3sc in next st, 3sc, slst in next st, skip the remaining sts. [11]

Fasten off, leaving a tail for sewing.

Insert the safety eyes in the centre of the orange eye pieces – poke a hole through the fabric with a knitting needle or scissors to loosen the stitches if this proves tricky. Secure the safety eyes at the back. **(photo 3)**

Head and body

Make 1, start in **Beige** yarn.

Round 1: 5sc in a magic ring. [5]

Round 2: Inc in all 5 sts. [10]

Rounds 3–4: Sc in all 10 sts. [2 rounds]

Round 5: 2sc, inc in next 6 sts, 2sc. [16]

Round 6: 2sc, (1sc, inc in next st) 6 times, 2sc. [22]

Round 7: 2sc, (inc in next st, 2sc) 6 times, 2sc. [28]

Round 8: 2sc, (3sc, inc in next st) 6 times, 2sc. [34]

Round 9: 2sc, (inc in next st, 4sc) 6 times, 2sc. [40]

Round 10: (4sc, inc in next st) 8 times. [48]

Round 11: (5sc, inc in next st) 8 times. [56]

Round 12: 7sc, (6sc, inc in next st) 7 times. [63] **(photo 4)**

Round 13: (10sc, inc in next st, 10sc) 3 times. [66]

Round 14: Sc in all 66 sts. [66]

Rounds 15–20: Change to **Brown** yarn held together with **Caramel Mohair** for extra fluffiness, sc in all 66 sts. [6 rounds] **(photo 5)**

Round 21: (10sc, inv dec, 10sc) 3 times. [63]

Rounds 22–24: Sc in all 63 sts. [3 rounds]

Round 25: (inv dec, 19sc) 3 times. [60] **(photo 6)**

Rounds 26–31: Sc in all 60 sts. [6 rounds]

Round 32: (9sc, inv dec, 9sc) 3 times. [57]

Rounds 33–34: Sc in all 57 sts. [2 rounds]

The next round marks the positions of the arms.

Round 35: 19sc, 3sc in next st, 36sc, 3sc in next st. [61]

Round 36: 20sc, 3sc in next st, 38sc, 3sc in next st, 1sc. [65] **(photo 7)**

Next, pin the two eye patches to the front of the face, so that the arm markings are on the bottom edge. Sew in place, adding a little stuffing under the orange part of each eye. **(photos 8 and 9)**

Round 37: 21sc, 3sc in next st, 40sc, 3sc in next st, 2sc. [69]

Round 38: 19sc, ch1, skip 7sts, 36sc, ch1, skip 7 sts. [57] **(photo 10)**

Rounds 39–40: Sc in all 57 sts. [2 rounds]

Round 41: (inv dec, 17sc) 3 times. [54]

Rounds 42–44: Sc in all 54 sts. [3 rounds]

Round 45: (8sc, inv dec, 8sc) 3 times. [51]

Rounds 46–48: Sc in all 51 sts. [3 rounds]

Round 49: (inv dec, 15sc) 3 times. [48]

The next round marks the positions of the legs.

Round 50: 2sc, ch7, skip next st, 14sc, ch7, skip next st, 30sc. [46 + 2 7ch gaps] **(photo 11)**

Round 51: 2sc, 7sc along the chain, 14sc, 7sc along the chain, 30sc. [60]

Round 52: 4sc, sc3tog, 18sc, sc3tog, 32sc. [56]

Round 53: 3sc, sc3tog, 16sc, sc3tog, 31sc. [52]

Round 54: 2sc, sc3tog, 14sc, sc3tog, 30sc. [48]

Round 55: (inv dec, 6sc) 6 times. [42]

Round 56: (5sc, inv dec) 6 times. [36] **(photo 12)**

Round 57: (2sc, inv dec, 2sc) 6 times. [30]

Round 58: (3sc, inv dec) 6 times. [24]

Add lots of toy stuffing.

Round 59: (1sc, inv dec, 1 sc) 6 times. [18]

Round 60: (1sc, inv dec) 6 times. [12]

Round 61: Inv dec 6 times. [6]

Fasten off, leaving a tail. Thread tail through front loops with a tapestry needle and pull tight to close. **(photo 13)**

Ears

Make 2 in **Beige** yarn.

Row 1: 5sc in a magic ring, turn. [5]

Row 2: Ch1, inc in all 5 sts, turn. [10]

Row 3: Ch1, sc in all 10 sts. [10]

Fasten off, leaving a tail for sewing. **(photo 14)**

Pin the ears to the top of the head, above the eyes between **Rounds 18 and 19**, approximately 15 stitches apart. Sew in place. **(photo 15)**

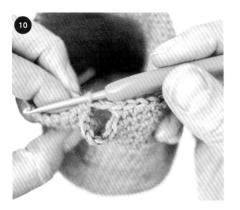

Arms and legs

Make 4, start in **Brown** yarn held together with **Caramel Mohair** yarn.

For the arms, join the yarn to the first of the skipped stitches. For the legs, join the yarn to the first of the new chains. **(photo 16)**

Round 1: 7sc along the skipped stitches/chains, 1sc into the side of the gap, 1sc into the stitch/chain on next row, 1sc into the other side of the gap. [10]

Rounds 2–7: Sc in all 10 sts. [6 rounds]

Round 8: Inv dec 3 times, 4sc. [7]

Round 9: 3slst, 1sc, inc 2 times, 1sc. [9]

Round 10: 3slst, 6sc. [9]

Rounds 11–28: Sc in all 9 sts. [18 rounds]

Round 29: (inv dec, 1sc) 2 times, 3sc. [7]

Round 30: Sc in all 7 sts. [7]

Fasten off and add some craft pipe cleaners (chenille stems) or wire into the arms and legs at this point if you choose to. Stitch the arms and legs closed. **(photo 17)**

Palms and fingers

Make 4 in **Beige** yarn.

Round 1: 7sc in a magic ring. [7]

Round 2: 2sc, (ch4, start 2nd ch from hook, 3slst into back humps of the chains, 1sc in next st) 5 times. [7 + 5 fingers] **(photo 18)**

Round 3: 2sc, (skip the chain, 1sc in next st) 5 times. [7]

Fasten off, leaving a tail for sewing. **(photo 19)**

Sew the palms to the arms and legs, positioning them so that the fingers point forwards. **(photo 20)**

Final details

Using **Brown** yarn, embroider a small nose and a smile to finish. **(photo 21)**

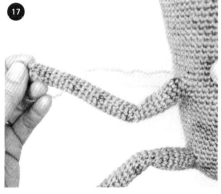

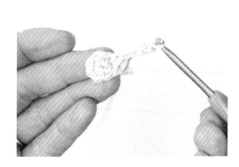

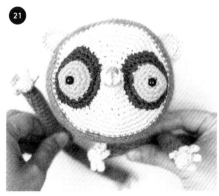

pufferfish

The pufferfish may not look like anything special most of the time, but just wait until it senses danger – by taking in extra water and air this fish can blow itself up into a giant, spiky ball! I'm sure to other ocean inhabitants this transformation is very intimidating, and the pufferfish safely bobs away from any unwanted encounters, but to the human eye, this transformation is rather comic: the tiny front fins fly up, the eyes are full of surprise, and the mouth is wide open – it's as if they can't quite believe what's just happened!

DIMENSIONS

12cm (5in) tall

YARNS

Paintbox Yarns Cotton DK (100% cotton) 125m (137yds) per 50g (1¾oz) ball:

- **Orange:** 1 x 50g (1¾oz) ball in Melon Sorbet (shade 417)

- **White:** 1 x 50g (1¾oz) ball in Champagne White (shade 403)

- **Pink:** 1 x 50g (1¾oz) ball in Blush Pink (shade 454)

HOOKS

3mm (US C/2 or D/3) hook

other tools and materials

- Pair 8mm black safety eyes
- Craft pipe cleaner (chenille stem) or wire
- Toy stuffing
- Sewing pins
- Tapestry needle

FUN FACT

The pufferfish is a secret artist. It spends over a week creating beautiful geometric circular nests in the sand on the sea floor.

Tension (gauge)

Tension is not critical for this project, but if you want to match the pattern shown, make a small circular swatch using the chosen yarn and hook (see Tools and materials: Tension swatch for the swatch pattern).

When made in DK weight cotton with a 3mm (US C/2 or D/3) hook the swatch should measure 3.5cm (1⅜in) across.

Project notes

The body is worked in one piece, with the mouth joined in as you go. The spikes are created at the same time as the body by working short sections of chain stitches and slip stitches. If you prefer to work the spikes separately and sew them on, simply skip them when making the body. The eyes, fins and tail are sewn onto the body at the end. The tail and fins are finished with a row of crab stitch to create a bumpy texture.

Special stitches

Back loop only (BLO): Insert the hook under the back loop only (see Crochet techniques: Front loops/back loops).

Spike: Ch5, start 2nd ch from hook, work in the back hump (3rd loop) of the chain, 4slst. [4]

Crab stitch (reverse single crochet): Working from left to right, insert hook into next st, yarn over, pull through to the front of the work, yarn over, pull through the 2 loops on hook.

Mouth

Make 1 in **Pink** yarn.

Round 1: 6sc in a magic ring. [6]

Round 2: Inc 6 times. [12]

Round 3: (1sc, inc in next st) 6 times. [18]

Round 4: (2sc, inc in next st) 6 times. [24]

Rounds 5–7: Sc in all 24 sts. [3 rounds]

You will need a piece of wire or a craft pipe cleaner (chenille stem) long enough to go around the mouth shape for the next part.

Round 8: Working in BLO, and over the wire, sc in all 24 sts. **(photo 1)**

Fasten off. Twist the ends of the wire together and trim off the excess. Turn the mouth wrong side out and set aside. **(photo 2)**

Body

Make 1, start in **Orange** yarn.

Round 1: 6sc in a magic ring. [6]

Round 2: Inc 6 times. [12]

From the next round, spikes (see Special stitches) will be added on some of the rounds. At the same time, each round is increased by 6 stitches. The spikes will not count in stitch totals for the rounds.

Round 3: (1sc, spike, inc in next st) 6 times. [18 + 6 spikes] **(photo 3)**

Round 4: (1sc, move the spike to the front of the work, 1sc, inc in next st) 6 times. [24] **(photo 4)**

Round 5: (3sc, inc in next st) 6 times. [30]

Round 6: (4sc, spike, inc in next st) 6 times. [36 + 6 spikes] **(photo 5)**

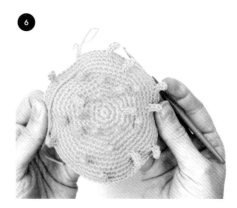

Round 7: (5sc, inc in next st) 6 times. [42]

Round 8: (6sc, inc in next st) 6 times. [48]

Round 9: (1sc, spike, 6sc, inc in next st) 6 times. [54 + 6 spikes]

Round 10: (8sc, inc in next st) 6 times. [60]

Round 11: (9sc, inc in next st) 6 times. [66]

Round 12: (5sc, spike, 5sc, inc in next st) 6 times. [72 + 6 spikes]

Rounds 13–14: Sc in all 72 sts. [2 rounds] **(photo 6)**

Round 15: 3sc, spike (6sc, spike) 11 times, 3sc. [72 + 12 spikes]

Rounds 16–18: Sc in all 72 sts. [3 rounds]

Round 19: 1sc, (spike, 6sc) 5 times, 12sc, (spike, 6sc) 4 times, spike, 5sc. [72 + 10 spikes] **(photo 7)**

Round 20: Sc in all 72 sts.

In the next round we will join in the mouth.

Round 21: 29sc, with the mouth piece wrong side out line it up with the body, work the next set of stitches through both body and the free front loops of **Round 8** of the mouth, **(photo 8)** 12sc, now work on body only, 31sc. [72] **(photo 9)**

The top half of the mouth is now attached.

Round 22: Change to **White**, 29sc, work the next set of stitches through the front loops of the bottom half of the mouth only, **(photo 10)** 12sc, skip the 12 stitches along the top of the mouth and carry on, working on the body only, 31sc. [72] **(photo 11)**

The mouth is now part of the body. Pinch it closed and carry on working in **White**. Fasten off **Orange** and trap the end under the next round to secure it.

Round 23: Sc in all 72 sts.

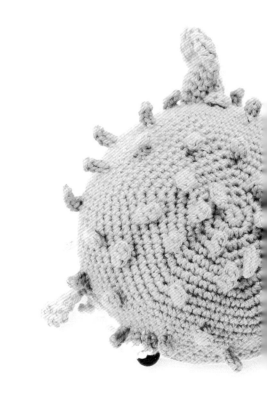

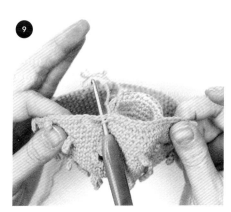

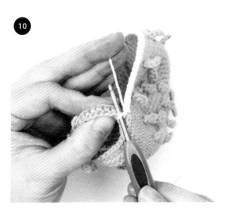

Round 24: 5sc, (spike, 6sc) 4 times, 18sc, (spike, 6sc) 4 times, spike, 1sc. [72 + 9 spikes] **(photo 12)**

Rounds 25–27: Sc in all 72 sts. [3 rounds]

Round 28: 3sc, (spike, 6sc) 11 times, spike, 3sc. [72 +12 spikes]

Rounds 29-30: Sc in all 72 sts. [2 rounds]

Round 31: (inv dec, 5sc, spike, 5sc) 6 times. [66 + 6 spikes]

Round 32: (inv dec, 9sc) 6 times. [60]

Round 33: (inv dec, 8sc) 6 times. [54]

Round 34: (inv dec, 7sc, spike) 6 times. [48 + 6 spikes]

Round 35: (inv dec, 6sc) 6 times. [42]

Round 36: (inv dec, 5sc) 6 times. [36]

Round 37: (inv dec, 2sc, spike, 2sc) 6 times. [30 + 6 spikes]

Round 38: (inv dec, 3sc) 6 times. [24]

Round 39: (inv dec, 2sc) 6 times. [18] **(photo 13)**

Add lots of toy stuffing, taking care to stuff above and below the mouth.

Round 40: (inv dec, 1sc, spike) 6 times. [12 + 3 spikes]

Round 41: Inv dec 6 times. [6]

Fasten off, leaving a tail. Thread tail through front loops with a tapestry needle and pull tight to close. **(photo 14)**

Flippers

Make 2 in **Orange** yarn.

Ch4, start 2nd ch from hook, work in rows.

Row 1: 3sc, turn. [3]

Row 2: Ch2 (does not count as st), 2hdc in each st, turn. [6]

Row 3: Ch2, (2hdc in next st, 1hdc) 3 times, do not turn. [9]

Row 4: Ch1, 4 crab st, skip 1 st, 3 crab st, 1slst. [8]

Fasten off, leaving a long tail for sewing.

Tail

Make 1 in **Orange** yarn.

Ch12, join with a slst to make a ring.

Round 1: 1sc in each ch. [12]

Round 2: (inc in next st, 5sc) 2 times. [14]

Round 3: (inc in next st, 6sc) 2 times. [16]

Round 4: (inc in next st, 7sc) 2 times. [18]

Now work in rows.

Row 5: Slst in next st, fold the piece flat and work along the top through both layers, ch2, 2hdc in each st, turn. [18]

Row 6: Ch2, hdc in all 18 sts, do not turn. [18]

Row 7: Ch1, (skip 1 st, 1 crab st in next st) 9 times. [9]

Fasten off, leaving a tail for sewing.

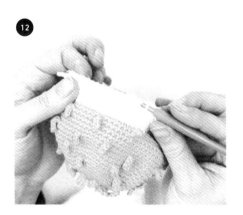

Eyes

Make 2, start in **White** yarn.

Round 1: 5sc in a magic ring. [5]

Round 2: Inc 5 times. [10]

Round 3: Change to **Orange**, work in front loops only, sc in all 10 sts. [10]

Round 4: 3slst, 4sc, 2slst, skip last st. [9]

Fasten off, leaving a tail for sewing.

Final details

Take the flippers and weave the yarn tails along the edge of the flippers, back to the starting chain. **(photo 15)**

Pin the flippers to the sides of the body along the colour change line – approximately 8 stitches away from the mouth corners – and sew in place (see Assembly techniques). **(photo 16)**

Take the finished tail and weave the yarn tail back to the starting chain. **(photo 17)**

Add a little stuffing **(photo 18)** and pin the tail to the back of the body, covering the colour jog from **Round 22**. Sew in place; for a neat seam, try sewing through the front posts of the stitches (see Assembly techniques). **(photo 19)**

Put the safety eyes through the eye pieces between **Rounds 1 and 2**. The safety eyes should be closer to the side of the crocheted eye with the slip stitches. **(photo 20)** If the eye stalk is too big make a hole between the rounds with a hook or the tip of some scissors.

Secure the eyes with the fasteners and pin them to the front of the body above the mouth corners. **(photo 21)** Sew the eyes in place through the front loops of the last round and weave in any loose ends to finish. **(photo 22)**

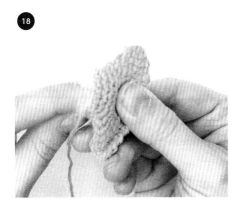

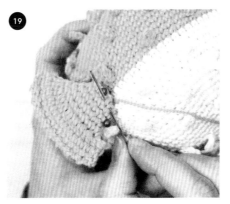

BLUE LOBSTER

Armed with impressive claws, wiggly legs and long antennae, lobsters are rather iconic sea dwellers. These amazing crustaceans are thought to never stop growing – just imagine a metre-long giant crawling along among the ancient shipwrecks! When we think of lobsters we tend to think of red, but they can be many different colours, from muddy brown to cerulean blue and even multicoloured. Contrary to the popular line from one well-known '90s sitcom, they do not actually mate for life ... never mind, plenty more fish in the sea!

DIMENSIONS

30cm (12in) long

YARNS

Paintbox Yarns Cotton DK (100% cotton), 125m (137yds) per 50g (1¾oz) ball:

- **Dark Blue:** 1 x 50g (1¾oz) ball in Sailor Blue (shade 440)

- **Blue:** 1 x 50g (1¾oz) ball in Dolphin Blue (shade 437)

- **Light Blue:** 1 x 50g (1¾oz) ball in Duck Egg Blue (shade 436)

HOOKS

3mm (US C/2 or D/3) hook

OTHER TOOLS AND MATERIALS

- Pair 10.5mm black safety eyes
- Toy stuffing
- Sewing pins
- Tapestry needle

FUN FACT

Lobsters have long lifespans, which allows them to reach impressive sizes. The largest lobster ever caught is thought to have weighed over 20kg (44lb)!

Tension (gauge)

Tension is not critical for this project, but if you want to match the pattern shown here, make a small circular swatch using the chosen yarn and hook (see Tools and materials: Tension swatch for the swatch pattern).

When made in DK weight cotton with a 3mm (US C/2 or D/3) hook the swatch should measure 3.5cm (1⅜in) across.

Project notes

The body is worked in one piece, from the nose down to the tail edge. The claws, antennae and legs are made separately and sewn to the body at the end. Using a range of tones of one colour creates a nice ombre effect – you could experiment with other shades for a more striking palette, perhaps a rainbow?

Body

Make 1, start in **Dark Blue** yarn.

Round 1: 6sc in a magic ring. [6]

Round 2: (1sc, inc in next st) 3 times. [9]

Round 3: (2sc, inc in next st) 3 times. [12]

Round 4: (3sc, inc in next st) 3 times. [15]

Round 5: (4sc, inc in next st) 3 times. [18]

Round 6: (5sc, inc in next st) 3 times. [21]

Round 7: (6sc, inc in next st) 3 times. [24]

Round 8: Sc in all 24 sts. [24]

Round 9: (7sc, inc in next st) 3 times. [27]

Round 10: Sc in all 27 sts. [27]

Round 11: (8sc, inc in next st) 3 times. [30]

Round 12: Sc in all 30 sts. [30]

Round 13: (9sc, inc in next st) 3 times. [33]

Round 14: Sc in all 33 sts. [33]

Round 15: (10sc, inc in next st) 3 times. [36]

Round 16: Sc in all 36 sts. [36] **(photo 1)**

The next round marks the positions of the eyes.

Round 17: (11sc, 3sc in next st) 2 times, 12sc. [40]

Round 18: 12sc, inc in next st, 13sc, inc in next st, 13sc. [42] **(photo 2)**

Rounds 19–22: Sc in all 42 sts. [4 rounds]

Round 23: Slst in all 42 sts. [42]

Round 24: (5sc, inc in next st) 7 times. [49]

Rounds 25–38: Sc in all 49 sts. [14 rounds]

Round 39: (inv dec, 5sc) 7 times. [42]

Round 40: (inv dec, 4sc) 7 times. [35]

Round 41: Slst in all 35 sts. [35]

Add the safety eyes between **Rounds 17 and 18**, where the increases are. The eyes now indicate the top side of the body. **(photo 3)**

Round 42: (4sc, inc in next st) 7 times. [42]

Rounds 43–45: Sc in all 42 sts. [3 rounds]

Round 46: (inv dec, 5sc) 6 times. [36]

Round 47: Slst in all 36 sts. [36]

Round 48: (5sc, inc in next st) 6 times. [42]

Rounds 49–51: Sc in all 42 sts. [3 rounds]

Round 52: (inv dec, 5sc) 6 times. [36]

Round 53: Slst in all 36 sts. [36] **(photo 4)**

Fasten off the **Dark Blue** yarn and join **Blue** to any slip stitch on the underside of the body.

Round 54: (5sc, inc in next st) 6 times. [42]

Rounds 55–56: Sc in all 42 sts. [2 rounds]

Round 57: (inv dec, 5sc) 6 times. [36]

Round 58: (inv dec, 10sc) 3 times. [33]

Round 59: Slst in all 33 sts. [33]

Round 60: (10sc, inc in next st) 3 times. [36]

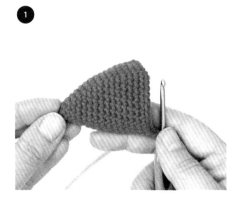

Rounds 61–63: Sc in all 36 sts. [3 rounds]

Round 64: (inv dec, 4sc) 6 times. [30]

Round 65: Slst in all 30 sts. [30] **(photo 5)**

Fasten off the **Blue** yarn and join **Light Blue** to any slip stitch on the underside of the body.

Round 66: (9sc, inc in next st) 3 times. [33]

Rounds 67–68: Sc in all 33 sts. [2 rounds]

Round 69: (inv dec, 9sc) 3 times. [30]

Round 70: (inv dec, 3sc) 6 times. [24] **(photo 6)**

Add lots of toy stuffing. Pinch the end flat so that the eyes are on the top half of the body.

Work additional sc until you reach a corner, then turn and work through both layers of the tail to close the gap.

Row 71: 12sc across the closed edge. [12] **(photos 7 and 8)**

Fasten off.

Antennae

Make 2 in **Dark Blue** yarn.

Round 1: 5sc in a magic ring. [5]

Rounds 2–42: Sc in all 5 sts. [41 rounds]

Fasten off, leaving a tail for sewing.
(photo 9)

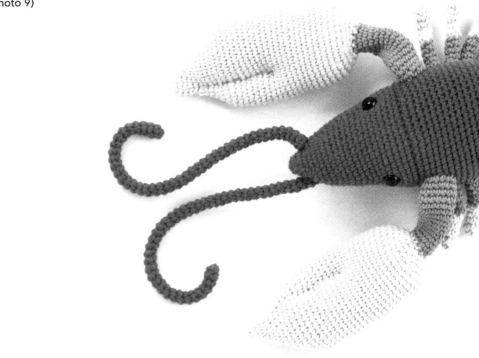

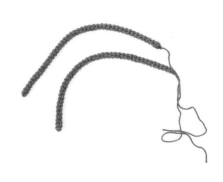

claws

Make 2, start in **Light Blue** yarn.

Round 1: 5sc in a magic ring. [5]

Round 2: 2sc, 3sc in next st, 2sc. [7]

Round 3: 3sc, 3sc in next st, 3sc. [9]

Round 4: 4sc, 3sc in next st, 4sc. [11]

Round 5: 5sc, 3sc in next st, 5sc. [13]

Round 6: 6sc, 3sc in next st, 6sc. [15]

Round 7: 7sc, 3sc in next st, 7sc. [17]

Round 8: 8sc, 3sc in next st, 8sc. [19]

Round 9: Inc in next st, 8sc, 3sc in next st, 8sc, inc in next st. [23]

Round 10: Inc in next st, 10sc, 3sc in next st, 10sc, inc in next st. [27]

Round 11: Inc in next st, 12sc, 3sc in next st, 12sc, inc in next st. [31]

Round 12: Inc in next st, 29sc, inc in next st. [33] **(photo 10)**

Rounds 13–32: Sc in all 33 sts. [20 rounds]

Round 33: (inv dec, 9sc) 3 times. [30]

Round 34: (3sc, inv dec) 6 times. [24]

Round 35: (2sc, inv dec) 6 times. [18]

Add toy stuffing.

Round 36: (1sc, inv dec) 6 times. [12]

Round 37: Slst in all 12 sts. [12] **(photo 11)**

Fasten off **Light Blue** and join **Blue** to any slip stitch. **(photo 12)**

Rounds 38–52: Sc in all 12 sts. [15 rounds] **(photo 13)**

Fasten off, leaving a tail for sewing.

Using a tapestry needle and the **Light Blue** yarn, stitch a line down each claw, dividing them into two. Use the increases from the start of **Round 9** as the starting point and sew up to **Round 20**. **(photo 14)**

Legs

Make 8, start in **Light Blue** yarn.

Round 1: 5sc in a magic ring. [5]

Rounds 2–5: Sc in all 5 sts. [4 rounds]

Round 6: 2sc, 3sc in next st, 2sc. [7]

Round 7: Change to **Blue** yarn, sc in all 7 sts. [7]

Round 8: 2sc, inv dec, 3sc. [6]

Rounds 9–11: Sc in all 6 sts. [3 rounds]

Fasten off, leaving a tail for sewing. **(photo 15)**

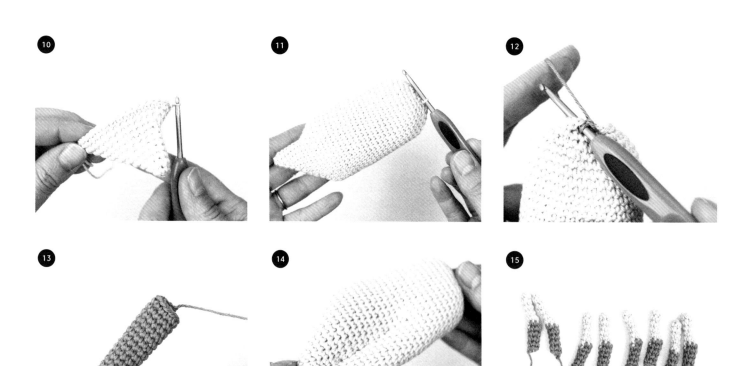

Tail

Make 1 in **Light Blue** yarn.

Round 1: 6sc in a magic ring. [6]

Round 2: (1sc, 3sc in next st, 1sc) 2 times. [10]

Round 3: (2sc, 3sc in next st, 2sc) 2 times. [14]

Round 4: Sc in all 14 sts. [14]

Round 5: (3sc, 5sc in next st, 3sc) 2 times. [22]

Round 6: (5sc, 3sc in next st, 5sc) 2 times. [26]

Round 7: (6sc, 3sc in next st, 6sc) 2 times. [30]

Rounds 8–9: Sc in all 30 sts. [2 rounds]

Round 10: (7sc, 5sc in next st, 7sc) 2 times. [38]

Round 11: (9sc, inc in next st, 9sc) 2 times. [40]

Rounds 12–14: Sc in all 40 sts. [3 rounds]

Round 15: (inv dec, 8sc) 4 times. [36]

Round 16: (inv dec, 7sc) 4 times. [32]

Round 17: (inv dec, 6sc) 4 times. [28]

Round 18: (inv dec, 5sc) 4 times. [24]

Fasten off, leaving a long tail for sewing and shaping. Add a little bit of stuffing.

Assembly

Place the tail over the flat end of the body and sew it into place using the posts of the stitches on either side of the flat end. **(photo 16)**

Using the **Light Blue** yarn, divide the tail into five segments with stitched seams, going from the body end of the tail to the tip, at the points where 5sc are worked into one stitch – these mark the segment tips for the tail. **(photos 17 and 18)**

Next, sew the claws to the sides of the body. **(photo 19)**

Sew the antennae to the tip of the nose. **(photo 20)**

Sew the legs to the underbelly to finish. **(photo 21)**

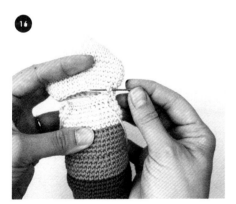

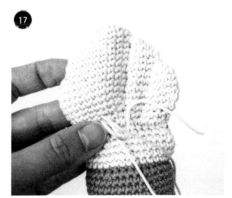

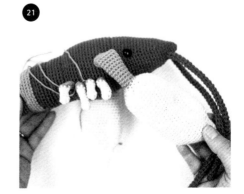

NARWHAL

Meet the elusive unicorn of the sea – need I say more! Narwhal
horns are simply spectacular, but what's even more intriguing is that
they aren't horns at all; in fact, they are more like an elephant's
tusk, growing like a giant tooth from one side of the mouth.
No one really knows what they use them for, and little is known
about narwhals in general, which, in my opinion, just adds to their
charm. Isn't it great there are still mysteries left to uncover?

Dimensions

40cm (15¾in) long

Yarns

Paintbox Yarns Cotton DK (100%
cotton), 125m (137yds) per 50g
(1¾oz) ball:

- **Light Grey:** 2 x 50g (1¾oz) balls in
  Misty Grey (shade 404)
- **Dark Grey:** 2 x 50g (1¾oz) balls in
  Slate Grey (shade 406)
- **White:** 2 x 50g (1¾oz) balls in
  Champagne White (shade 403)

Alternatively, you could make the
narwhal in hand-dyed speckled yarn
or Rico Ricorumi Spray DK Cotton in
Blue (shade 006)

Hooks

3mm (US C/2 or D/3) hook

Other tools and materials

- Pair 8mm black safety eyes
- Craft pipe cleaner (chenille stem)
- Small piece of thick felt or fabric
  stabilizer
- Toy stuffing
- Sewing pins
- Tapestry needle

FUN FACT

A narwhal's tusk can grow
up to 3m (9ft) long and
their skin is packed with
as much Vitamin C as an
orange gram for gram!

Tension (gauge)

Tension is not critical for this project, but if you want to match the pattern shown here, make a small circular swatch using the chosen yarn and hook (see Tools and materials: Tension swatch for the swatch pattern).

When made in DK weight cotton with a 3mm (US C/2 or D/3) hook the swatch should measure 3.5cm (1⅜in) across.

Project notes

The body of the narwhal is worked in one piece from the tip to the tail, mixing different shades of grey to create a speckled look.

Body

Make 1, start in **Dark Grey** yarn.

Round 1: 5sc in a magic ring. [5]

Round 2: Inc 5 times. [10]

Round 3: (1sc, inc in next st) 5 times. [15]

Round 4: (2sc, inc in next st) 5 times. [20]

Round 5: (3sc, inc in next st) 5 times. [25]

Round 6: (4sc, inc in next st) 5 times. [30]

Round 7: (5sc, inc in next st) 5 times. [35]

Round 8: (6sc, inc in next st) 5 times. [40]

Round 9: (7sc, inc in next st) 5 times. [45]

Round 10: (8sc, inc in next st) 5 times. [50]

Round 11: (9sc, inc in next st) 5 times. [55]

Round 12: (10sc, inc in next st) 5 times. [60] **(photo 1)**

Rounds 13–15: Sc in all 60 sts. [3 rounds] **(photo 2)**

Now add a few stripes of **Light Grey** to give your narwhal a fierce expression (optional). Catch the unused colours under the stitches or float them at the back.

Round 16: Change to **Light Grey**, sc in all 60 sts. [60]

Rounds 17–18: Change to **Dark Grey**, sc in all 60 sts. [2 rounds]

Round 19: Change to **Light Grey**, sc in all 60 sts. [60]

Round 20: Change to **Dark Grey**, sc in all 60 sts. [60] **(photo 3)**

Fasten off **Dark Grey** and continue in **Light Grey**. The next round adds a chain section that will become the mouth.

Round 21: Ch18, skip 12 sts, 48sc. [66] **(photo 4)**

Round 22: 18sc along the ch, working into the back humps, 48sc. [66] **(photo 5)**

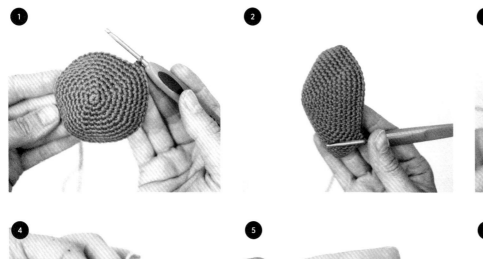

Round 23: Sc in all 66 sts. [66]

Round 24: (4sc, inv dec) 3 times, 48sc. [63]

Round 25: Sc in all 63 sts. [63]

Round 26: (inv dec, 3sc) 3 times, 48sc. [60] **(photo 6)**

Rounds 27–32: Sc in all 60 sts. [6 rounds]

Round 33: (inv dec, 2sc) 3 times, 48sc. [57]

Round 34: Sc in all 57 sts. [57]

Round 35: (inv dec, 1sc) 3 times, 48sc. [54]

Rounds 36–50: Sc in all 54 sts. [15 rounds]

Round 51: (4sc, inv dec) 3 times, 36sc. [51]

Round 52: Sc in all 51 sts. [51]

Round 53: (3sc, inv dec) 3 times, 36sc. [48]

Round 54: Sc in all 48 sts. [48]

Round 55: (2sc, inv dec) 3 times, 36sc. [45]

Rounds 56–57: Sc in all 45 sts. [2 rounds]

Round 58: (1sc, inv dec) 3 times, 36sc. [42]

Rounds 59–62: Sc in all 42 sts. [4 rounds]

Round 63: 2sc, inv dec 3 times, 34sc. [39]

Rounds 64–66: Sc in all 39 sts. [3 rounds]

Round 67: (inv dec, 11sc) 3 times. [36]

Round 68: Sc in all 36 sts. [36]

Round 69: (inv dec, 10sc) 3 times. [33]

Round 70: Sc in all 33 sts. [33]

Round 71: (inv dec, 9sc) 3 times. [30]

Round 72: Sc in all 30 sts. [30]

Round 73: (inv dec, 8sc) 3 times. [27]

Round 74: Sc in all 27 sts. [27]

Round 75: (inv dec, 7sc) 3 times. [24]

Round 76: Sc in all 24 sts. [24]

Round 77: (inv dec, 6sc) 3 times. [21]

Round 78: Sc in all 21 sts. [21]

Round 79: (inv dec, 5sc) 3 times. [18]

Round 80: Sc in all 18 sts. [18]

Round 81: (inv dec, 4sc) 3 times. [15]

Round 82: Sc in all 15 sts. [15]

Round 83: (inv dec, 3sc) 3 times. [12]

Round 84: Sc in all 12 sts. [12]

Round 85: Inv dec 6 times. [6]

Fasten off, leaving a tail. Thread tail through front loops with a tapestry needle and pull tight to close. **(photo 7)**

Add safety eyes on either side of the mouth opening. **(photo 8)**

Add lots of toy stuffing to the body shape.

Fold the mouth opening over the top section of the head up to the first **Light Grey** line and sew it into place, keeping the line of the mouth semi-circular. **(photo 9)**

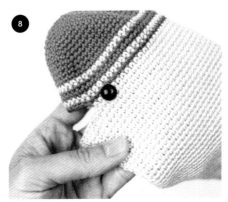

Flippers

Make 2 in **Light Grey** yarn.

Round 1: 5sc in a magic ring. [5]

Round 2: Sc in all 5 sts. [5]

Round 3: 2sc, 3sc in next st, 2sc. [7]

Round 4: 3sc, 3sc in next st, 3sc. [9]

Round 5: 4sc, 3sc in next st, 4sc. [11]

Round 6: 5sc, 3sc in next st, 5sc. [13]

Round 7: 6sc, 3sc in next st, 6sc. [15]

Round 8: 7sc, 3sc in next st, 7sc. [17]

Round 9: 8sc, 3sc in next st, 8sc. [19]

Round 10: 9sc, inc in next st, 9sc. [20]

Rounds 11–15: Sc in all 20 sts. [5 rounds]

Round 16: 7sc, inv dec 3 times, 7sc. [17]

Round 17: 6sc, inv dec, 1sc, inv dec, 6sc. [15]

Round 18: 5sc, inv dec, 1sc, inv dec, 5sc. [13]

Round 19: 5sc, inv dec, 6sc. [12]

Round 20: Sc in all 12 sts. [12]

Fasten off, leaving a tail for sewing. **(photo 10)**

Flatten the shape down the decrease lines and add a little stuffing.

Sew the flippers to the sides of the body, in line with the eyes. **(photo 11)**

Tail tips

Make 2, start in **Dark Grey** yarn.

Round 1: 5sc in a magic ring. [5]

Round 2: Sc in all 5 sts. [5]

Round 3: 2sc, 3sc in next st, 2sc. [7]

Round 4: 3sc, 3sc in next st, 3sc. [9]

Round 5: 4sc, 3sc in next st, 4sc. [11]

Round 6: 5sc, 3sc in next st, 5sc. [13]

Round 7: 6sc, 3sc in next st, 6sc. [15]

Round 8: 7sc, 3sc in next st, 7sc. [17]

Round 9: 8sc, 3sc in next st, 8sc. [19]

Round 10: 9sc, 3sc in next st, 9sc. [21]

Round 11: Sc in all 21 sts. [21]

Fasten off the first tail tip. Make the second tail tip but do not fasten off. **(photo 12)**

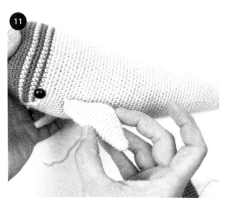

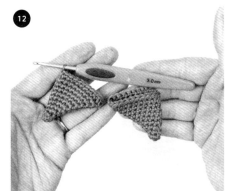

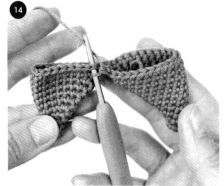

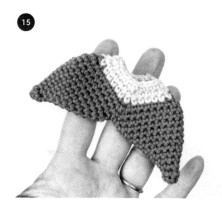

Joining the tail

Carry on in **Dark Grey** yarn.

Round 1: 11sc, bring first tail tip next to the second so that the increase lines are in the middle, 21sc along the second tail tip, then work the remaining stitches, 10sc, on the first tip. [42] **(photos 13 and 14)**

Round 2: Sc in all 42 sts. [42]

Round 3: (inv dec, 7sc, sc3tog, 7sc, inv dec) 2 times. [34]

Round 4: Change to **Light Grey**, (inv dec, 5sc, sc3tog, 5sc, inv dec) 2 times. [26]

Round 5: Sc in all 26 sts. [26]

Round 6: (inv dec, 3sc, sc3tog, 3sc, inv dec) 2 times. [18]

Fasten off, leaving a tail for sewing. **(photo 15)**

Cut a small piece of fabric stabilizer so that it matches the shape of the tail and insert it into the tail. **(photo 16)**

Place the tail over the tip of the body and sew it in place. **(photo 17)**

TUSK

Make 1 in **White** yarn.

Round 1: 5sc in a magic ring. [5]

Rounds 2–5: Sc in all 5 sts. [4 rounds]

Round 6: Inc in next st, 4sc. [6]

Rounds 7–9: Sc in all 6 sts. [3 rounds]

Round 10: Inc in next st, 5sc. [7]

Rounds 11–13: Sc in all 7 sts. [3 rounds]

Round 14: Inc in next st, 6sc. [8]

Rounds 15–17: Sc in all 8 sts. [3 rounds]

Round 18: Inc in next st, 7sc. [9]

Rounds 19–21: Sc in all 9 sts. [3 rounds]

Round 22: Inc in next st, 8sc. [10]

Rounds 23–25: Sc in all 10 sts. [3 rounds]

Round 26: Inc in next st, 9sc. [11]

Rounds 27–29: Sc in all 11 sts. [3 rounds]

Round 30: Inc in next st, 10sc. [12]

Fasten off, leaving a tail for sewing. Insert a craft pipe cleaner (chenille stem) into the tusk. Embroider a spiral around the tusk in thin strands of both **Light Grey** and **Dark Grey** to decorate. **(photos 18 and 19)**

Sew the tusk to the front of the body between **Rounds 6 and 10**. **(photo 20)**

Final details

Embroider the narwhal's back with little v-stitches in both **Light Grey** and **Dark Grey** yarns, blending in the stripes. **(photo 21)**

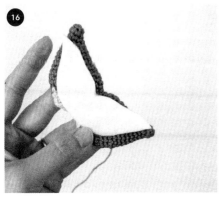

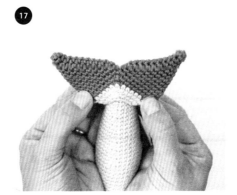

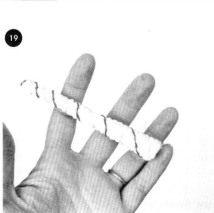

OCTOPUS

What has no bones, blue blood, three hearts and eight arms? An octopus, of course! A fluid, moving tangle of tentacles with many, many suckers, this beautiful animal is hard to wrap one's head around. Absent are the familiar markers of a well-defined head and body – we are looking at something else entirely. Masters of camouflage, octopuses can blend into any terrain. These clever predators can also solve complex puzzles, regrow a lost arm, squeeze through the tiniest of gaps and disappear in a puff of inky 'smoke' too – they are better escape artists than Houdini!

Dimensions

50cm (20in) long

Yarns

Paintbox Yarns Cotton DK (100% cotton) 125m (137yds) per 50g (1¾oz) ball:

- **Lilac:** 3 x 50g (1¾oz) balls in Tea Rose (shade 443)

- **Pale Purple:** 1 x 50g (1¾oz) ball in Dusty Rose (shade 442)

- **Dark Purple:** 1 x 50g (1¾oz) ball in Pansy Purple (shade 448)

Hooks

3mm (US C/2 or D/3) hook

Other tools and materials

- Pair 30mm clear safety eyes
- Craft pipe cleaners (chenille stems) or wire (optional)
- Removable stitch markers
- Toy stuffing
- Sewing pins
- Tapestry needle

FUN FACT

The octopus is a master of disguise. It can change the colour, and even texture, of its skin to blend in with its surroundings.

Tension (gauge)

Tension is not critical for this project, but if you want to match the pattern shown, make a small circular swatch using the chosen yarn and hook (see Tools and materials: Tension swatch for the swatch pattern).

When made in DK weight cotton with a 3mm (US C/2 or D/3) hook the swatch should measure 3.5cm (1⅜in) across.

Project notes

The body is worked in one piece, from the back down to the tentacles. The sucker caps on the tentacles are worked as a separate piece, and the whole underside is sewn to the body. Using large, clear eyes over a colourful yarn creates a beautiful eye colour. To finish, the back of the body is decorated with embroidery in different light and dark coordinating colours.

Special stitches

Popcorn: Ch3, 7dc in the 3rd ch from the hook, remove the hook and place it through the top of the beg 3-ch from the back of the work to the front, grab the last loop and pull it through the ch on the hook (1 popcorn made). Usually the hook is placed from the front to the back, but working it the opposite way gives a nice open look to the cluster.

Half-popcorn: Ch2, 5hdc in the 2nd ch from the hook, remove the hook and place it through the top of the beg 2-ch from the back of the work to the front, grab the last loop and pull it through the ch on the hook (1 half-popcorn made).

Picot: Ch3, slst in 1st ch.

Eyes

Make 2, start in **Pale Purple** yarn.

Ch6, join with a slst to make a ring. [6]

Round 1: Inc in each ch. [12]

Round 2: (1sc, inc in next st) 6 times. [18]

Round 3: (2sc, inc in next st) 6 times. [24]

Change to **Dark Purple**, fasten off **Pale Purple**.

Rounds 4–6: Sc in all 24 sts. [3 rounds]

Change to **Lilac**, fasten off **Dark Purple**.

Round 7: (inc in next st, 1dc) 12 times. [36]

Rounds 8–9: Sc in all 36 sts. [2 rounds]

Fasten off, leaving a long tail for sewing. **(photo 1)**

Place the clear eye through the starting ring, but do not fasten yet. Set aside. **(photo 2)**

Body

Make 1 in **Lilac** yarn.

Round 1: 6sc in a magic ring. [6]

Round 2: Inc 6 times. [12]

Round 3: (1sc, inc in next st) 6 times. [18]

Round 4: (2sc, inc in next st) 6 times. [24]

Round 5: (3sc, inc in next st) 6 times. [30]

Round 6: (4sc, inc in next st) 6 times. [36]

Round 7: (5sc, inc in next st) 6 times. [42]

Round 8: (6sc, inc in next st) 6 times. [48]

Round 9: (7sc, inc in next st) 6 times. [54]

Round 10: (8sc, inc in next st) 6 times. [60]

Round 11: (9sc, inc in next st) 6 times. [66]

Round 12: (10sc, inc in next st) 6 times. [72]

Round 13: (11sc, inc in next st) 6 times. [78]

Round 14: (12sc, inc in next st) 6 times. [84]

Round 15: (13sc, inc in next st) 6 times. [90]

Rounds 16–30: Sc in all 90 sts. [15 rounds] **(photo 3)**

The next section has decreases along one side of the body; each round is decreased by 3 stitches until there are 42 stitches in total.

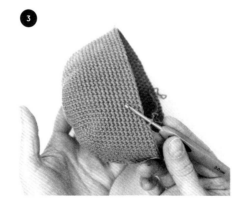

Round 31: 30sc, (inv dec, 18sc) 3 times. [87]

Round 32: 30sc, (inv dec, 17sc) 3 times. [84]

Round 33: 30sc, (inv dec, 16sc) 3 times. [81]

Round 34: 30sc, (inv dec, 15sc) 3 times. [78]

Round 35: 30sc, (inv dec, 14sc) 3 times. [75]

Round 36: 30sc, (inv dec, 13sc) 3 times. [72]

Round 37: 30sc, (inv dec, 12sc) 3 times. [69]

Round 38: 30sc, (inv dec, 11sc) 3 times. [66]

Round 39: 30sc, (inv dec, 10sc) 3 times. [63]

Round 40: 30sc, (inv dec, 9sc) 3 times. [60]

Round 41: 30sc, (inv dec, 8sc) 3 times. [57]

Round 42: 30sc, (inv dec, 7sc) 3 times. [54]

Round 43: 30sc, (inv dec, 6sc) 3 times. [51]

Round 44: 30sc, (inv dec, 5sc) 3 times. [48]

Round 45: 30sc, (inv dec, 4sc) 3 times. [45]

Round 46: 30sc, (inv dec, 3sc) 3 times. [42] **(photo 4)**

Rounds 47–51: Sc in all 42 sts. [5 rounds]

In the next round, two holes are added for eye placement. If you prefer to skip this step, crochet in the same way as for the previous round.

Round 52: 2sc, ch1, skip next st, 20sc, ch1, skip next st, 18sc. [42] **(photo 5)**

Round 53: 2sc, 1sc over the ch, 20sc, 1sc over the ch, 18sc. [42]

Rounds 54–58: Sc in all 42 sts. [5 rounds]

Round 59: 30sc, (3sc, inc in next st) 3 times. [45]

Round 60: 30sc, (4sc, inc in next st) 3 times. [48]

Increases for the tentacles begin in the next round.

Round 61: (2sc, inc in next st, 3sc) 8 times. [56]

Round 62: (3sc, 3sc in next st, 3sc) 8 times. [72]

Round 63: (4sc, 3sc in next st, 4sc) 8 times. [88] **(photo 6)**

Round 64: (inv dec, 3sc, 3sc in next st, 3sc, inv dec) 8 times. [88]

Round 65: (5sc, 3sc in next st, 5sc) 8 times. [104]

Round 66: (inv dec, 4sc, 3sc in next st, 4sc, inv dec) 8 times. [104]

Round 67: (6sc, 3sc in next st, 6sc) 8 times. [120] **(photo 7)**

Add safety eyes to the gaps from **Round 52**, secure with fasteners. **(photos 8 and 9)**

Round 68: (inv dec, 5sc, 3sc in next st, 5sc, inv dec) 8 times. [120]

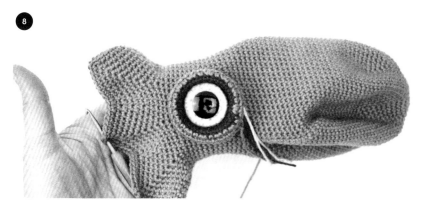

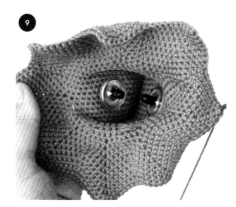

Round 69: (7sc, 3sc in next st, 7sc) 8 times. [136]

Round 70: (inv dec, 6sc, 3sc in next st, 6sc, inv dec) 8 times. [136]

In the next round, the gaps for 8 tentacles are created.

Round 71: 7sc, place stitch marker in last worked st, 4sc, (ch1, skip next 12 sts, 5sc) 7 times, ch1, skip next 6sts. [54] **(photo 10)**

Round 72: Skip 6 sts to get to marked st (5sc, 1sc over the chain) 8 times. [48] **(photo 11)** Slst in next st, fasten off. We will return to this round and close the shape after making the tentacles.

Using a tapestry needle, sew the outer edge of the eyes to the body. **(photo 12)**

Add stuffing to the body up to the level of the safety eyes.

Tentacles

Make 8 in **Lilac** yarn.

Join in yarn just before the first stitch of any 12-stitch gap created in **Round 69** of the body.

Round 1: 12sc, 3sc across the gap. [15] **(photo 13)**

Rounds 2–16: Sc in all 15 sts. [15 rounds]

Round 17: (inv dec, 3sc) 3 times. [12]

Rounds 18–32: Sc in all 12 sts [15 rounds]

Round 33: (inv dec, 2sc) 3 times. [9]

Rounds 34–48: Sc in all 9 sts. [15 rounds]

Round 49: (inv dec, 1sc) 3 times [6]

Rounds 50–64: Sc in all 6 sts. [15 rounds]

Fasten off, leaving a tail. Thread tail through front loops with a tapestry needle and pull tight to close. **(photo 14)**

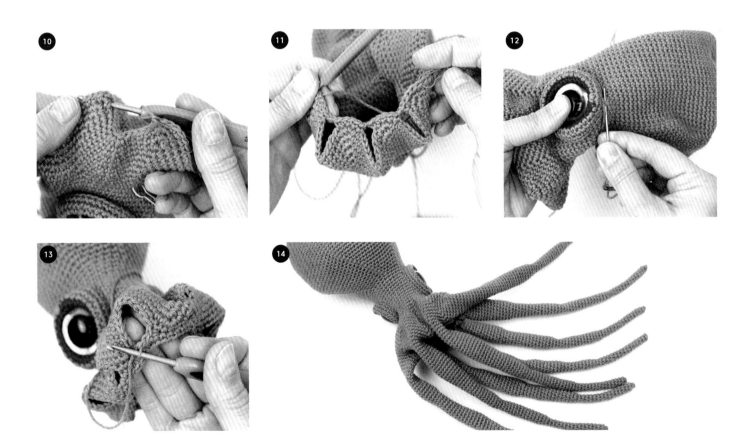

Insert some wire or craft pipe cleaners (chenille stems) into each tentacle at this point if you choose to and stuff them lightly. If using pipe cleaners, twist two together first for extra strength. Add stuffing to the body. **(photo 15)**

underside

Make 1 in **Lilac** yarn.

Join yarn to any stitch from **Round 70** of the body.

Round 1: (6sc, inv dec) 6 times. [42]

Round 2: (4sc, inv dec) 7 times. [35]

Round 3: (3sc, inv dec) 7 times. [28]

Round 4: (2sc, inv dec) 7 times. [21]

Top up the body stuffing, filling out the shape.

Round 5: (1sc, inv dec) 7 times. [14]

Round 6: Inv dec 7 times. [7]

Fasten off, leaving a tail. Thread tail through front loops with a tapestry needle and pull tight to close. **(photo 16)**

underside decoration

Make in **Pale Purple** yarn.

Round 1: 8sc in a magic ring. [8]

Round 2: Inc in all 8 sts. [16]

Round 3: (1sc, inc in next st) 8 times. [24]

Round 4: (1sc, 3sc in next st, 1sc) 8 times. [40]

Round 5: (inv dec, 3sc in next st, inv dec) 8 times. [40]

Round 6: (2sc, 3sc in next st, 2sc) 8 times. [56]

Round 7: (inv dec, 1sc, 3sc in next st, 1sc, inv dec) 8 times. [56]

Round 8: (3sc, 3sc in next st, 3sc) 8 times. [72] **(photo 17)**

The next round is a bit tricky: long strings of popcorn and picot stitches are added to make up the undersides of the tentacles. They will give a neat sucker-like appearance once pressed. Don't worry if your chain of popcorns twists, it will be straightened when it's slip-stitched back down from the tentacle tips.

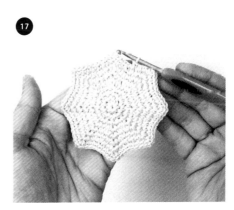

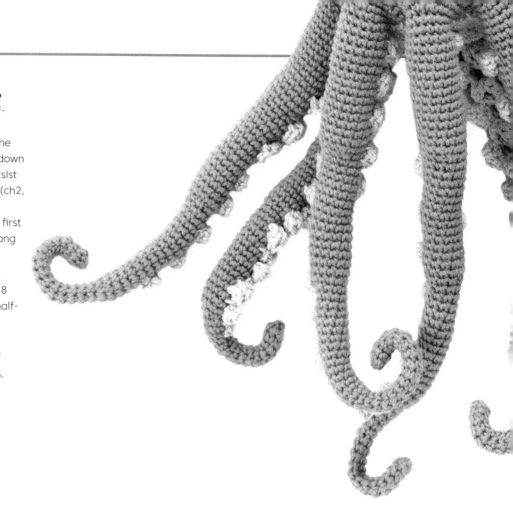

Tentacle round: 5sc, popcorn, **(photo 18)** (ch2, popcorn) 9 times, (ch2, half-popcorn) 9 times, (ch4, slst in 2nd ch from hook) 3 times, this is the tip of the tentacle. **(photo 19)** Now work back down to the middle: slst in next 5ch, (ch1, 2slst between the half-popcorns) 9 times, (ch2, 2slst between the popcorns) 9 times, **(photos 20–22)** ch2, slst into the very first ch at the start of the tentacle, 4sc along the main round. **(photos 23 and 24)**

Repeat **Tentacle round** 7 more times, creating 8 tentacle undersides. [72 + 8 tentacles, each with 10 popcorns, 9 half-popcorns and 3 picots]

Fasten off, leaving a long tail for sewing. Press your finger into each of the popcorns to open out the suckers. **(photo 25)**

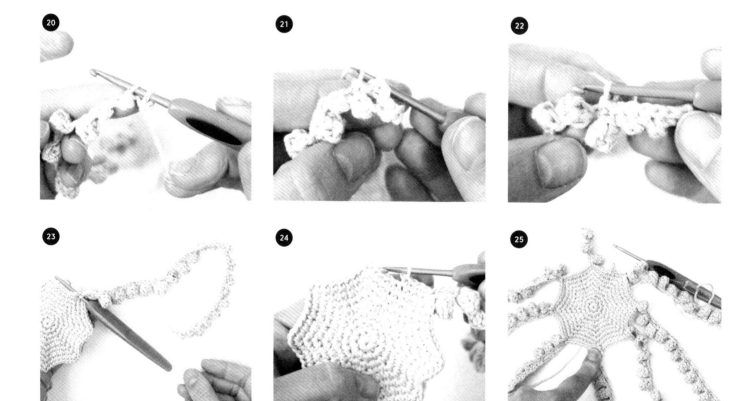

Assembly

Turn the octopus upside down and pin the underside to the bottom of the body, matching the positions of the tentacles. **(photo 26)**

Carefully start stitching the two together – whip stitch will work well (see Assembly techniques). To start, go along the central crochet base, then up one side of a tentacle. You can do this by eye, or you could secure the tentacles with removable stitch markers. Don't worry if something is uneven, it will have a natural look.

Secure the back of the popcorns to the main tentacle, alternating their positions from left to right. Try working up to the tip of the tentacle along the right-hand side, catching every other popcorn, then working back down to the body on the left-hand side catching the other popcorns. **(photos 27–29)**

Final details

Once the underside is attached embroider some spots to the top of the body, alternating colours at random. **(photos 30 and 31)**

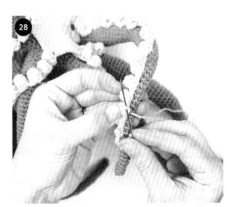

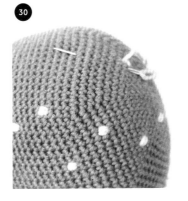

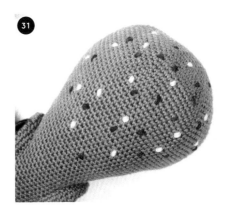

LEAFY SEA DRAGON

This mysterious leafy sea dragon blends so well into the kelp forest – blink and you'll swim right past it! A relative of seahorses, it moves around using two tiny fins near the front of the head. And, just like seahorses, the males are responsible for incubating the eggs and looking after the mini sea dragons – neat! Some say legendary dragons were inspired by these sea beauties moving gracefully in the waves.

DIMENSIONS

50cm (20in) long

YARNS

Paintbox Yarns Cotton DK (100% cotton), 125m (137yds) per 50g (1¾oz) ball:

- **Bright Yellow:** 1 x 50g (1¾oz) ball in Daffodil Yellow (shade 422)
- **Light Yellow:** 1 x 50g (1¾oz) ball in Banana Cream (shade 421)

HOOKS

3mm (US C/2 or D/3) hook

Other tools and materials

- Pair 6mm black safety eyes
- Craft pipe cleaner (chenille stem) or wire
- Toy stuffing
- Sewing pins
- Tapestry needle

FUN FACT

The leafy sea dragon has no known predators thanks to its perfect camouflage, protective bony plates and the sharp spines on its side.

Tension (gauge)

Tension is not critical for this project, but if you want to match the pattern shown here, make a small circular swatch using the chosen yarn and hook (see Tools and materials: Tension swatch for the swatch pattern).

When made in DK weight cotton with a 3mm (US C/2 or D/3) hook the swatch should measure 3.5cm (1⅜in) across.

Project notes

This project explores the use of increases and decreases to create the wobbly line of the sea dragon's body. The leaf-like appendages are added onto the base, with some embroidery to finish.

Head and body

Make 1 in **Bright Yellow** yarn.

Round 1: 6sc in a magic ring. [6]

Round 2: Inc 6 times. [12]

Round 3: Sc in all 12 sts. [12]

Round 4: 3sc, (inc in next st, 1sc) 3 times, 3sc. [15]

Round 5: Sc in all 15 sts. [15]

Round 6: 3sc, inv dec 5 times, 2sc. [10]

Rounds 7–13: Sc in all 10 sts. [7 rounds]

Round 14: Slst in all 10 sts. [10] **(photo 1)**

Round 15: (1sc, inc in next st) 5 times. [15]

Round 16: 9sc, 3sc in next st, 3sc, 3sc in next st, 1sc. [19]

Round 17: 10sc, 3sc in next st, 5sc, 3sc in next st, 1sc. [22] **(photo 2)**

Round 18: 15sc, 3sc in next st, 7sc. [25]

Round 19: 10sc, inv sc3tog, 3sc, 3sc in next st, 3sc, inv sc3tog, 2sc. [23] **(photo 3)**

Round 20: 4sc, inc in next st, 4sc, inv sc3tog, 3sc, 3sc in next st, 3sc, inv sc3tog, 1sc. [22]

Round 21: 15sc, 3sc in next st, 6sc. [24]

Round 22: 16sc, inc in next st, 7sc. [25]

Add safety eyes between the increases on **Rounds 16 and 17. (photo 4)**

Round 23: 15sc, inv dec, 1sc, inv dec, 5sc. [23]

Round 24: 14sc, inv dec, 1sc, inv dec, 4sc. [21]

Round 25: 13sc, inv dec, 1sc, inv dec, 3sc. [19]

Round 26: 4sc, inc 2 times, 6sc, inv dec, 1sc, inv dec, 2sc. [19]

Round 27: 5sc, inc 2 times, 6sc, (inv dec, 1sc) 2 times. [19]

Round 28: 6sc, inc 2 times, 6sc, inv dec, 1sc, inv dec. [19]

Add stuffing to the nose and head. **(photo 5)**

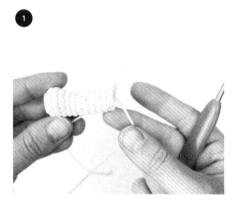

Round 29: 7sc, inc 2 times, 7sc, inc in next st, 1sc, inc in next st. [23]

Round 30: 9sc, inc 2 times, 12sc. [25]

Rounds 31–35: Sc in all 25 sts. [5 rounds]

Round 36: Inv dec, 20sc, inv dec, 1sc. [23]

Round 37: Inv dec, 18sc, inv dec, 1sc. [21]

Round 38: Inv dec, 16sc, inv dec, 1sc. [19]

Round 39: Inv dec, 14sc, inv dec, 1sc. [17]

Round 40: Inv dec, 12sc, inv dec, 1sc. [15]

Add stuffing up to this point. **(photo 6)**

Round 41: Inc in next st, 5sc, inc 2 times, 5sc, inc in next st, 1sc. [19]

Round 42: 8sc, inc 2 times, 9sc. [21]

Round 43: 9sc, inc 2 times, 10sc. [23]

Rounds 44–46: Sc in all 23 sts. [3 rounds]

Round 47: 10sc, inv dec 2 times, 9sc. [21]

Round 48: 9sc, inv dec 2 times, 8sc. [19]

Round 49: 8sc, inv dec 2 times, 7sc. [17]

Round 50: Inv dec, 5sc, inv dec 2 times, 6sc. [14]

Add stuffing up to this point and then stuff as you go. **(photo 7)**

Round 51: Inv dec, 12sc. [13]

Round 52: Inv dec, 11sc. [12]

Round 53: Inv dec, 10sc. [11]

Round 54: Inv dec, 9sc. [10]

Round 55: Inv dec, 8sc. [9]

Round 56: Inv dec, 7sc. [8]

Round 57: Sc in all 8 sts. [8]

Round 58: Inv dec, 6sc. [7]

Round 59: Sc in all 7 sts. [7]

Round 60: Inv dec, 5sc. [6]

Rounds 61–70: Sc in all 6sts. [10 rounds]

Fasten off, leaving a tail. Insert a craft pipe cleaner (chenille stem) into the tail of the sea dragon. Thread yarn tail through front loops with tapestry needle and pull tight to close. **(photo 8)**

Large leaves

Make 8 (4 for each side) or more, start in **Bright Yellow** yarn.

Ch13, start 2nd ch from hook, work in the back humps.

Row 1: Sc in all 12 ch, fasten off **Bright Yellow**. [12]

Now work **Row 2A** or **Row 2B** depending on which side the leaf is for.

Attach **Light Yellow** to the first chain, work around both sides.

Row 2A (right side): Ch1, 2slst, 1sc, ch4, start 2nd ch from hook, 3sc along the chain, 3sc along main row, ch5, start 2nd ch from hook, 4sc along the chain, 3sc along main row, ch6, start 2nd ch from hook, (1sc, 1hdc, 3sc) along the chain, 1sc, 1hdc, 1dc, (3dc, 1hdc) into the chain at the end of the main row, working on the other side of the chain 8sc, 4slst. **(photo 9)**

Fasten off, leaving a tail for sewing.

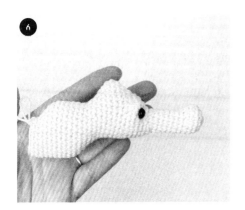

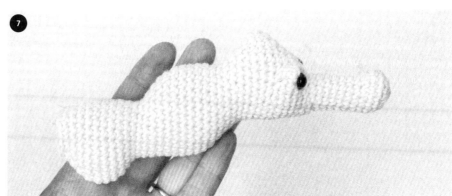

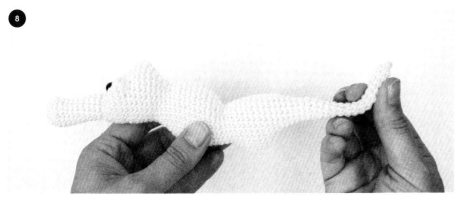

Row 2B (left side): Ch1, 4slst, 8sc, (1hdc, 3dc) into the chain at the end of the main row, working along the other side of the chain 1dc, 1hdc, 1sc, ch6, start 2nd ch from hook, (1sc, 1hdc, 3sc) along the chain, 3sc along main row, ch5, start 2nd ch from hook, 4sc along the chain, 3sc along the main row, ch4, start 2nd ch from hook, 3sc along the chain, (1sc, 2slst) along the main row.

Fasten off, leaving a tail for sewing. **(photo 10)**

Medium leaves

Make 4 in **Light Yellow** yarn.

Ch8, start 2nd ch from hook, work in the back hump.

Row 1: 1sc, 2hdc, 1sc, ch3, start 2nd ch from hook, 2sc along the chain, 1sc along main chain, 2slst.

Fasten off, leaving a tail for sewing. **(photo 11)**

Small leaves

Make 4 in **Light Yellow** yarn.

Ch6, start 2nd ch from hook, work in the back hump.

Row 1: 1sc, 1hdc, 1sc, 2slst. [5]

Fasten off, leaving a tail for sewing. **(photo 12)**

Pectoral fins

Make 2 in **Light Yellow** yarn.

Ch6, start 3rd ch from hook, work in the back hump.

Row 1: 2dc in next ch, 1dc, 2dc in next ch, skip next ch, slst in last ch. [6]

Fasten off, leaving a tail for sewing.

Dorsal fin

Make 1 in **Light Yellow** yarn.

Ch10, start 3rd ch from hook, work in the back hump.

Row 1: (2dc in next ch, 1dc) 3 times, 2dc in each next 2sts. [13]

Fasten off, leaving a tail for sewing. **(photo 13)**

Assembly

Arrange the large leaves along the body, sewing them down in pairs: two pairs on the top, two pairs on the bottom. **(photos 14 and 15)**

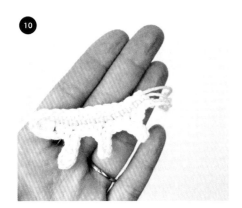

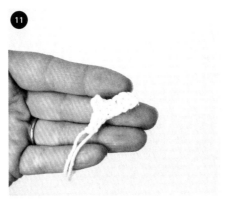

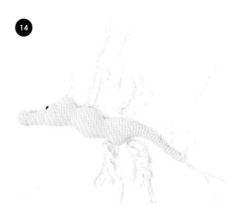

Sew the dorsal fin to the back. **(photo 16)**

Sew the pectoral fins to either side of the head. **(photo 17)**

Sew one set of small and medium leaves along the tail, the smallest closest to the tip. **(photo 18)**

Sew one set of medium leaves close together at the peak of the head.

Sew the last set of small leaves to the underside of the body. **(photo 19)**

Final details

Embroider around the eyes in **Light Yellow**, and decorate the body with stripes if you want to add more details. **(photos 20 and 21)**

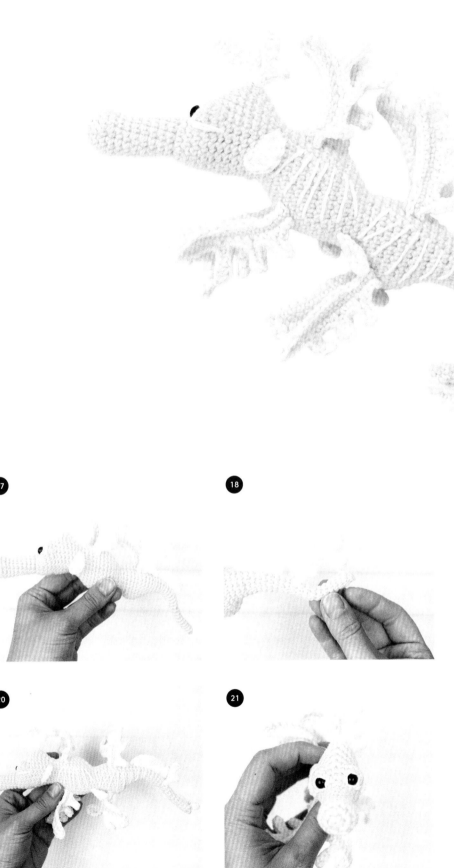

CASSOWARY

Have you ever wondered what it would feel like to stand next to a dinosaur? Look no further than the rather impressive cassowary: strong powerful legs, long sharp talons, a colourful face and a thick head crest – it is often called the most dangerous bird in the world! But these two-metre (six feet) tall, feathered giants prefer a diet of tropical fruit – which they swallow whole in one gulp – and a quiet, secluded life, walking in the forest; they really are a beautiful sight to behold!

Dimensions

35cm (13¾in) tall

Yarns

Paintbox Yarns Cotton DK (100% cotton), 125m (137yds) per 50g (1¾oz) ball:

- **Blue:** 1 x 50g (1¾oz) ball in Sailor Blue (shade 440)
- **Dark Grey:** 1 x 50g (1¾oz) ball in Slate Grey (shade 406)
- **Light Blue:** 1 x 50g (1¾oz) ball in Marine Blue (shade 434)
- **Red:** 1 x 50g (1¾oz) ball in Pillar Red (shade 415)
- **Orange:** 1 x 50g (1¾oz) ball in Melon Sorbet (shade 417)
- **Black 1 (feathers):** 1 x 50g (1¾oz) ball in Pure Black (shade 402)

DMC Natura Just Cotton 4-ply (100% cotton), 155m (170yds) per 50g (1¾oz) ball:

- **Black 2 (feathers):** 1 x 50g (1¾oz) ball in Noir (shade 11)

HOOKS

3mm (US C/2 or D/3) hook

Other tools and materials

- Pair 10.5mm black safety eyes
- Craft pipe cleaners (chenille stems) or wire (optional)
- Small piece of thick felt or fabric stabilizer
- Tapestry needle
- Toy stuffing
- Sewing pins

FUN FACT

The cassowary is an emotional character. It can change the colour of its head and neck depending on what kind of mood it's in.

Tension (gauge)

Tension is not critical for this project, but if you want to match the pattern shown here, make a small circular swatch using the chosen yarn and hook (see Tools and materials: Tension swatch for the swatch pattern).

When made in DK weight cotton with a 3mm (US C/2 or D/3) hook the swatch should measure 3.5cm (1⅜in) across.

Project notes

The head, neck and body of the cassowary are worked in one piece from the top down. The feathers are added after assembly. Using a combination of different black yarns creates a more interesting texture – and you can use up all your scraps of black yarn here too!

Eyes

Make 2 in **Orange** yarn.

Round 1: 5sc in a magic ring. [5]

Round 2: Inc in all 5 sts. [10]

Fasten off, leaving a tail for sewing.

Insert the safety eyes through the centre of the eyes but don't fasten the backs. Set aside for now. **(photo 1)**

Head, neck and body

Make 1, start in **Light Blue** yarn.

Round 1: 6sc in a magic ring. [6]

Round 2: Inc in all 6 sts. [12]

Round 3: (3sc, inc 3 times) 2 times. [18]

Round 4: 3sc, (1sc, inc in next st) 3 times, 3sc, (1sc, inc in next st) 3 times. [24]

Round 5: 3sc, (inc in next st, 2sc) 3 times, 3sc, (inc in next st, 2sc) 3 times. [30]

Round 6: 3sc, (3sc, inc in next st) 3 times, 3sc, (3sc, inc in next st) 3 times. [36]

Round 7: 3sc, (inc in next st, 4sc) 3 times, 3sc, (inc in next st, 4sc) 3 times. [42]

Round 8: 3sc, (5sc, inc in next st) 3 times, 3sc, (5sc, inc in next st) 3 times. [48]

Rounds 9–12: Sc in all 48 sts. [4 rounds]

Round 13: 15sc, change to **Blue**, 33sc. [48]

Fasten off **Light Blue**.

Rounds 14–15: Sc in all 48 sts. [2 rounds] **(photo 2)**

Round 16: 3sc, (inv dec, 5sc) 3 times, 24sc. [45]

Round 17: 3sc, (4sc, inv dec) 3 times, 24sc. [42]

Round 18: 3sc, (inv dec, 3sc) 3 times, 24sc. [39]

Round 19: 3sc, (2sc, inv dec) 3 times, 24sc. [36]

Round 20: 3sc, (inv dec, 1sc) 3 times, 24sc. [33]

Round 21: 3sc, inv dec 3 times, 24sc. [30]

Add the safety eyes (already inserted in the **Orange** circles) between **Rounds 13 and 14**, arranging them on the half of the head with the decreases, about 15 stitches apart. **(photo 3)**

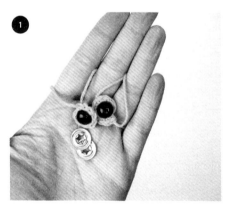

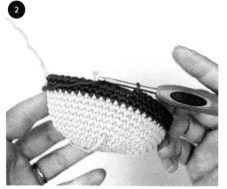

Round 22: (8sc, inv dec) 3 times. [27]

Rounds 23–46: Sc in all 27 sts. [24 rounds] (photo 4)

Round 47: 21sc, 6slst. [27]

Now start the increases for the body.

Round 48: 21sc, inc 6 times. [33]

Round 49: (6sc, inc in next st) 3 times, 12sc. [36]

Round 50: 24sc, (inc in next st, 1sc) 6 times. [42]

Round 51: (7sc, inc in next st) 3 times, 18sc. [45]

Round 52: 30sc, (inc in next st, 1sc) 6 times, 3sc. [51]

Round 53: (8sc, inc in next st) 3 times, 24sc. [54]

Round 54: (inc in next st, 8sc) 6 times. [60]

Rounds 55–62: Sc in all 60 sts. [8 rounds]

Add toy stuffing to the head and neck. (photo 5)

Round 63: 6sc, (inv dec, 6sc) 3 times, 30sc. [57]

Round 64: 6sc, (5sc, inv dec) 3 times, 30sc. [54]

Round 65: 6sc, (inv dec, 4sc) 3 times, 30sc. [51]

Round 66: 6sc, (3sc, inv dec) 3 times, 30sc. [48]

Round 67: 6sc, (inv dec, 2sc) 3 times, 30sc. [45]

Round 68: 6sc, (1sc, inv dec) 3 times, 30sc. [42]

Round 69: (4sc, inv dec) 7 times. [35]

Round 70: (3sc, inv dec) 7 times. [28]

Round 71: (2sc, inv dec) 7 times. [21]

Add lots of toy stuffing to the body.

Round 72: (1sc, inv dec) 7 times. [14]

Round 73: Inv dec 7 times. [7]

Fasten off, leaving a tail. Thread tail through front loops with a tapestry needle and pull tight to close. (photo 6)

BEAK

First make 2 pieces in **Dark Grey** yarn, then join them together.

Round 1: 5sc in a magic ring. [5]

Rounds 2–3: Sc in all 5 sts. [2 rounds]

Round 4: 2sc, 3sc in next st, 2sc. [7]

Round 5: Sc in all 7 sts. [7]

Round 6: 3sc, 3sc in next st, 3sc. [9]

Round 7: Sc in all 9 sts. [9]

Round 8: 4sc, 3sc in next st, 4sc. [11]

Round 9: Sc in all 11 sts. [11]

Round 10: 5sc, 3sc in next st, 5sc. [13]

Round 11: Sc in all 13 sts. [13]

Round 12: 6sc, 3sc in next st, 6sc. [15]

Round 13: Sc in all 15 sts. [15]

Fasten off one piece. Make the second piece, then carry on joining the two together as you work. (photos 7, 8, 9 and 10)

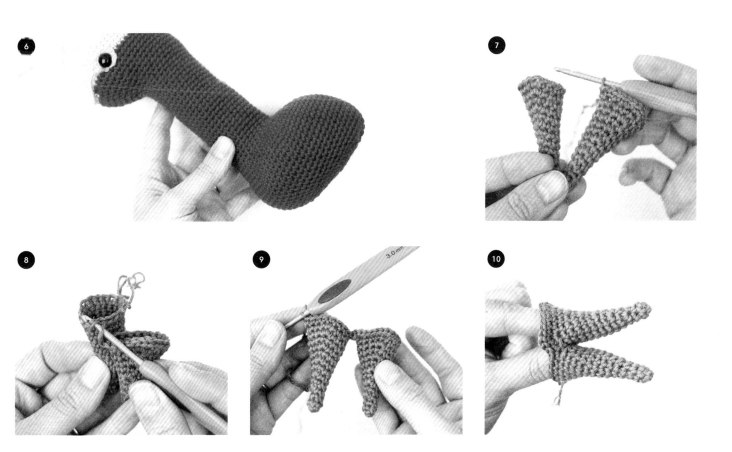

Round 14: 3sc (do not count as stitches in the total), (3sc in next st, 3sc) 2 times, 3sc in next st, bring the first piece next to the second (the one you're working on), skip first 3 sts of the first piece, 9sc along the first piece, skip the last 3 sts. [24]

Round 15: Start this round in the first stitch of the first increases from **Round 14**, 1sc, (3sc in next st, 5sc) 2 times, 10sc. [27]

Fasten off, leaving a tail for sewing.

Cut two thin triangles of fabric stabilizer and insert them into each beak section. Sew up the middle section. **(photos 11 and 12)**

Head crest

Make 1 in **Dark Grey** yarn.

Round 1: 6sc in a magic ring. [6]

Round 2: (1sc, 3sc in next st, 1sc) 2 times. [10]

Round 3: (2sc, 3sc in next st, 2sc) 2 times. [14]

Round 4: (3sc, 3sc in next st, 3sc) 2 times. [18]

Round 5: (4sc, 3sc in next st, 4sc) 2 times. [22]

Round 6: 5sc, 3sc in next st, 16sc. [24]

Round 7: 6sc, 3sc in next st, 17sc. [26]

Round 8: 7sc, 3sc in next st, 18sc. [28]

Round 9: 8sc, 3sc in next st, 19sc. [30]

Round 10: 9sc, 3sc in next st, 20sc. [32]

Round 11: 10sc, 3sc in next st, 21sc. [34]

Round 12: 11sc, 3sc in next st, 22sc. [36]

Round 13: 12sc, 3sc in next st, 23sc. [38]

Round 14: 13sc, 3sc in next st, 24sc. [40]

Round 15: Sc in all 40 sts. [40]

Fasten off, leaving a tail for sewing. Press flat along the increase line. Cut a matching shape from some thick felt or fabric stabilizer. For a better fit, cut a curve along the longest edge of the stabilizer piece, matching the curve of the top of the head. **(photos 13 and 14)**

Place the stabilizer inside the crest and add a little stuffing on either side of it. **(photo 15)**

Pin the beak over the front of the head, covering up the colour change line, with the triangular section at the top. Sew it into place. **(photos 16 and 17)**

Pin the crest to the top of the head with the tip overlapping the top of the beak. Sew it into place. **(photo 18)**

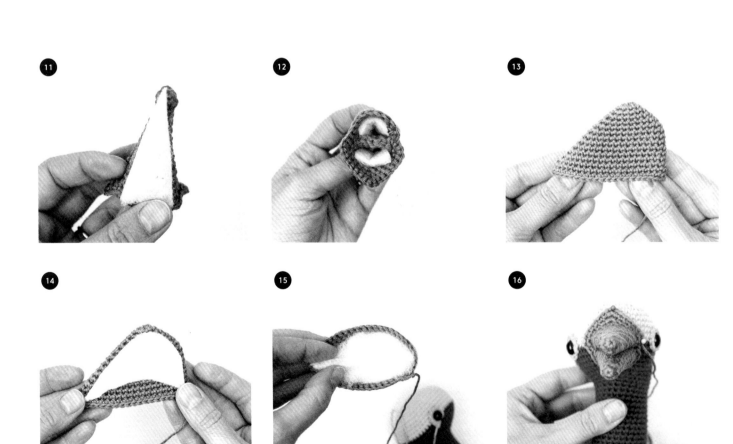

wattles

Make 2, start in **Red** yarn.

Round 1: 5sc in a magic ring. [5]

Round 2: Inc in all 5 sts. [10]

Round 3: (1sc, inc in next st) 5 times. [15]

Rounds 4–5: Sc in all 15 sts. [2 rounds]

Round 6: (inv dec, 3sc) 3 times. [12]

Rounds 7–8: Change to **Blue**, sc in all 12 sts. [2 rounds]

Round 9: (inv dec, 2sc) 3 times. [9]

Rounds 10–17: Sc in all 9 sts. [8 rounds]

Fasten off, leaving a tail for sewing. Add a little stuffing into the base. **(photo 19)**

Sew the two wattles to the top of the neck between **Rounds 24 and 27**. **(photo 20)**

Feet

Make 2 in **Dark Grey** yarn.

Round 1: 6sc in a magic ring. [6]

Round 2: Inc in all 6 sts. [12]

Round 3: (1sc, inc in next st) 6 times. [18]

Round 4: 3sc, (1sc, 3sc in next st, 1sc) 3 times, 3sc, inv sc3tog. [22] **(photo 21)**

Round 5: 3sc, (2sc, 3sc in next st, 2sc) 3 times, 4sc. [28]

Round 6: 3sc, (3sc, 3sc in next st, 3sc) 3 times, 4sc. [34]

Round 7: 3sc, (4sc, 3sc in next st, 4sc) 3 times, 4sc. [40]

Round 8: 3sc, (4sc, inv sc3tog, 4sc) 3 times, 4sc. [34]

Round 9: 3sc, (3sc, inv sc3tog, 3sc) 3 times, 4sc. [28]

Round 10: 3sc, (2sc, inv sc3tog, 2sc) 3 times, 4sc. [22]

Round 11: 3sc, (1sc, inv sc3tog, 1sc) 3 times, 4sc. [16]

Round 12: Sc in all 16 sts. [16]

Round 13: (2sc, inv dec) 4 times. [12]

Rounds 14–15: Sc in all 12 sts. [2 rounds]

Cut out a shape to match the footprint of the foot from stabilizer and insert it into the foot. Top up the stabilizer with some toy stuffing. **(photo 22)**

Round 16: (2sc, inv dec) 3 times. [9]

Rounds 17–26: Sc in all 9 sts. [10 rounds]

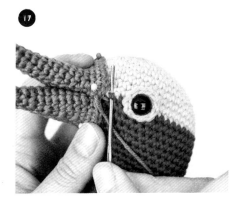

The next few rounds create the knee bend.

Round 27: 4sc, 3sc in next st, 4sc. [11]

Round 28: 5sc, 3sc in next st, 5sc. [13]

Round 29: 6sc, 3sc in next st, 6sc. [15]

Round 30: Sc in all 15 sts. [15]

Round 31: 6sc, inv sc3tog, 6sc. [13]

Round 32: 6sc, inv dec, 5sc. [12]

Rounds 33–36: Sc in all 12 sts. [4 rounds]

Fasten off, leaving a tail for sewing. At this point you could insert some wire or craft pipe cleaners (chenille stems) into the leg, but this is optional. Add some stuffing. **(photo 23)**

ASSEMBLY

Pin the legs to the base of the body, slightly forwards of the centre. Sew them in place with the knees pointing to the back of the body. **(photos 24 and 25)**

Next add the feathers. To do this you can use any **Black** yarn; a combination of 4-ply and DK weights creates a nice uneven texture. If you keep your yarn tail scraps you could add in any black scraps too!

Cut a bunch of **Black** yarn into 15cm (6in) pieces. Fold them in half and hook them through the fabric of the body. **(photo 26)**

Now hook the two tails through the loop to secure each strand. **(photos 27 and 28)**

Keep adding strands of **Black** yarn all over until your cassowary is covered in feathers. Brush it out with a hairbrush and trim any strands that are too long. **(photos 29 and 30)**

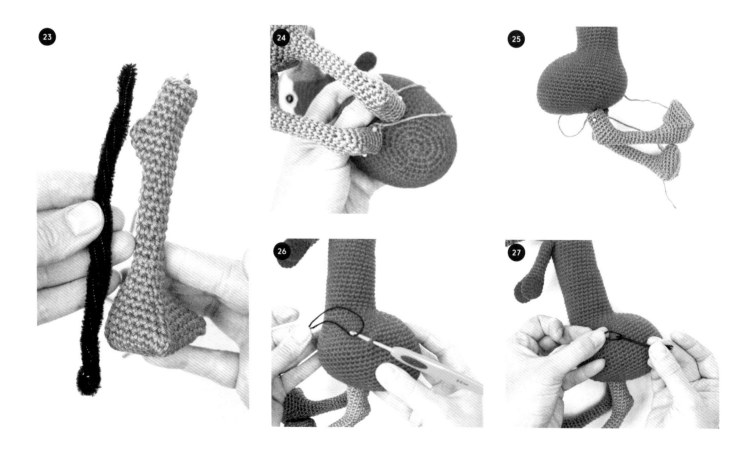

Final details

If you want to add more details, you could embroider the inside of the beak in **Red** yarn. **(photo 31)**

Using **Black** yarn, embroider a claw onto each toe.Start by working longer horizontal stitches over the same spot in the fabric, then change to vertical stitches and work only over the stitches just done, then change again to horizontal stitches and work over the vertical stitches, each time adding a little less thread than before. Create each claw in this way until you are happy with them. **(photos 32 and 33)**

FLAMINGO

So flexible, so slender, so elegant and oh so delightfully pink! I must confess I have a bit of an obsession with flamingos, their beautiful feathers and their unusual poses. These birds start out as fluffy grey chicks, only developing their pink plumage as they grow. Interestingly, the colour of their feathers comes from the food they eat; their favourite snack contains the same pigment that makes carrots orange. Their legs are usually longer than their entire body, and no one is sure exactly why they like to stand on one leg!

DIMENSIONS

40cm (15¾in) tall

YARNS

Paintbox Yarns Cotton DK (100% cotton), 125m (137yds) per 50g (1¾oz) ball:

- **Bright Pink:** 2 x 50g (1¾oz) balls in Bubblegum Pink (shade 451)
- **Black:** 1 x 50g (1¾oz) ball in Pure Black (shade 402)
- **Pale Blue:** 1 x 50g (1¾oz) ball in Seafoam Blue (shade 432)
- **Pale Pink:** 1 x 50g (1¾oz) ball in Candyfloss Pink (shade 450)

Rowan Kidsilk Haze Lace Weight Mohair (70% mohair, 30% silk), 210m (230yds) per 25g (1oz) ball:

- **Pink Mohair:** 1 x 25g (1oz) ball in Sweet (shade 688)

HOOKS

3mm (US C/2 or D/3) hook

3.5mm (US E/4) hook

OTHER TOOLS AND MATERIALS

- Pair 6mm black safety eyes
- 3 long pieces of thick gardening wire for the legs and neck (optional)
- Toy stuffing
- Sewing pins
- Tapestry needle

FUN FACT

A group of flamingos is called a flamboyance! Flamingos can be found in the wild in Florida, Central and South America and Africa.

Tension (gauge)

Tension is not critical for this project but if you want to match the pattern shown here, make a small circular swatch using the chosen yarn and hook (see Tools and materials: Tension swatch for the swatch pattern).

When made in DK weight cotton with a 3mm (US C/2 or D/3) hook the swatch should measure 3.5cm (1⅜in) across. When made with DK weight cotton and lace weight mohair held together with a 3.5mm (US E/4) hook the swatch should measure 4cm (1⅝in) across.

Project notes

The flamingo's head and neck are worked in one piece; the curves are created by skipping stitches and hidden chains. To make the flamingo's body extra fluffy a chain stitch texture in lace weight pink mohair is added over the top. The legs and neck can be reinforced with wire so that the flamingo can be posed. The head, neck and body of the flamingo could be worked in a faux fur or boucle yarn instead of the combined yarns.

Special stitches

Front loop only (FLO): Insert the hook under the front loop only (see Crochet techniques: Front loops/back loops).

Beak

Make 1, start in **Black** yarn with a 3mm (US C/2 or D/3) hook.

Round 1: 5sc in a magic ring. [5]

Round 2: 2sc, 3sc in next st, 2sc. [7]

Round 3: 3sc, 3sc in next st, 3sc. [9]

Round 4: 4sc, 3sc in next st, 4sc. [11]

Round 5: 5sc, 3sc in next st, 5sc. [13]

Round 6: 6sc, 3sc in next st, 6sc. [15]

Round 7: 7sc, 3sc in next st, 7sc. [17]

Round 8: 8sc, 3sc in next st, 8sc. [19]

Round 9: 9sc, 3sc in next st, 9sc. [21]

Round 10: 10sc, 3sc in next st, 10sc. [23]

Round 11: 11sc, 3sc in next st, 11sc. [25]

Round 12: 12sc, 3sc in next st, 12sc. [27]

Round 13: 11sc, inv dec, 1sc, inv dec, 6sc, 5slst. [25]

Round 14: 5slst, 7sc, inv dec, 11sc. [24]

Round 15: Sc in all 24 sts. [24]

Rounds 16–23: Change to **Pale Blue** yarn, sc in all 24 sts. [8 rounds]

Round 24: 2sc, slst in next st, skip the remaining sts. [3]

Fasten off, leaving a tail for sewing. **(photo 1)**

Head

Make 1 in **Bright Pink** yarn held together with **Pink Mohair**, with a 3.5mm (US E/4) hook.

Round 1: 7sc in a magic ring. [7]

Round 2: Inc in all 7 sts. [14]

Round 3: (1sc, inc in next st) 7 times. [21]

Round 4: (2sc, inc in next st) 7 times. [28]

Round 5: (3sc, inc in next st) 7 times. [35]

Round 6: (4sc, inc in next st) 7 times. [42]

Round 7: (6sc, inc in next st) 6 times. [48]

Rounds 8–9: Sc in all 48 sts. [2 rounds]

Round 10: 3sc in next st, 47sc. [50]

Round 11: 1sc, 3sc in next st, 48sc. [52]

Round 12: 2sc, 3sc in next st, 49sc. [54]

Round 13: 3sc, 3sc in next st, 50sc. [56] **(photo 2)**

Rounds 14–15: Sc in all 56 sts. [2 rounds]

Next, we will divide the head and neck.

Round 16: 53sc, ch7, skip 3 sts. [53 + 7ch]

Round 17: Skip 12 sts, 41sc, 7sc along the chain. [48] **(photo 3)**

Round 18: Sc in all 48 sts. [48]

Round 19: (inv dec, 6sc) 6 times. [42]

Round 20: (inv dec, 4sc) 7 times. [35]

Round 21: (inv dec, 3sc) 7 times. [28]

Round 22: (inv dec, 2sc) 7 times. [21]

Round 23: (inv dec, 1sc) 7 times. [14]

Round 24: Inv dec 7 times. [7]

Fasten off, leaving a tail. Thread tail through front loops with a tapestry needle and pull tight to close.

Add the safety eyes between **Rounds 12 and 13**, approximately 14 stitches apart. Add toy stuffing to the head. **(photo 4)**

Neck and body

Carry on in **Bright Pink** yarn held together with **Pink Mohair**, with a 3.5mm (US E/4) hook.

Join the yarn to the first st of the 7ch gap on the head.

Round 1: 7sc along the chain, 15sc along the free stitches from **Rounds 16 and 17**. [22]

Rounds 2-12: Sc in all 22 sts. [11 rounds] **(photo 5)**

The next section adds some subtle bends to the neck. **(photo 6)**

Round 13: 2sc, ch8, skip 8sts, 12sc. [22]

Round 14: 2sc, tuck the chain inside the work, 8sc along the skipped sts from previous round, 12sc. [22]

Round 15: 1sc, ch10, skip 10 sts, 11sc. [22]

Round 16: 1sc, tuck the chain inside of the work, 10sc along the skipped sts from previous round, 11sc. [22]

Round 17: Ch12, skip 12 sts, 10sc. [22]

Round 18: Tuck the chain inside the work, 12sc along the skipped sts from previous round, 10sc. [22]

Start adding stuffing as you go.

Rounds 19-36: Sc in all 22 sts. [18 rounds]

Round 37: 5sc, inc in next st, 10sc, inc in next st, 5sc. [24]

Round 38: Sc in all 24 sts. [24]

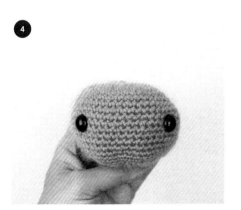

In the next section, a curve is added that begins the body. Insert a length of wire into the neck if you want it to be fully poseable.

Round 39: 3sc in next st, 23sc. [26]

Round 40: 1sc, 3sc in next st, 24sc. [28]

Round 41: 2sc, 3sc in next st, 25sc. [30] **(photo 7)**

Round 42: Ch7, skip 7 sts, 1sc, (6sc, inc in next st) 3 times, 1sc. [33]

Round 43: Tuck the chain inside the work, work into skipped sts from last round, 3sc, 3sc in next st, 3sc, 26sc. [35] **(photo 8)**

Round 44: Ch9, skip 9 sts, 1sc, (inc in next st, 7sc) 3 times, 1sc. [38]

Round 45: Tuck the chain inside the work, work into skipped sts from last round, 4sc, 3sc in next st, 4sc, 29sc. [40]

Round 46: Ch11, skip 11 sts, 1sc, (8sc, inc in next st) 3 times, 1sc. [43]

Round 47: Tuck the chain inside the work, work into skipped sts from last round, 5sc, 3sc in next st, 5sc, 32sc. [45] **(photo 9)**

Round 48: 6sc, 3sc in next st, 38sc. [47]

Round 49: 7sc, 3sc in next st, 39sc. [49]

Round 50: 8sc, 3sc in next st, 40sc. [51]

Round 51: 9sc, 3sc in next st, 41sc. [53]

Round 52: 10sc, 3sc in next st, 42sc. [55]

Round 53: 11sc, 3sc in next st, 43sc. [57]

Round 54: 12sc, 3sc in next st, 44sc. [59]

Round 55: 13sc, 3sc in next st, 45sc. [61]

Round 56: 14sc, 3sc in next st, 46sc. [63] **(photo 10)**

Round 57: 12sc in FLO, 7sc in both loops, 44sc. [63]

Rounds 58–59: Sc in all 63 sts. [2 rounds]

Round 60: 13sc, inv dec, 1sc, inv dec, 13sc, (inv dec, 6sc) 4 times. [57]

Round 61: 12sc, inv dec, 1sc, inv dec, 40sc. [55]

Round 62: 11sc, inv dec, 1sc, inv dec, 11sc, (5sc, inv dec) 4 times. [49]

Round 63: 10sc, inv dec, 1sc, inv dec, 34sc. [47]

Round 64: 9sc, inv dec, 1sc, inv dec, 9sc, (inv dec, 6sc) 3 times. [42]

Round 65: (inv dec, 4sc) 7 times. [35]

Round 66: (3sc, inv dec) 7 times. [28]

Round 67: (inv dec, 2sc) 7 times. [21]

Add lots of stuffing to the body. **(photo 11)**

Round 68: (1sc, inv dec) 7 times. [14]

Round 69: Inv dec 7 times. [7]

Fasten off, leaving a tail. Thread tail through front loops with a tapestry needle and pull tight to close.

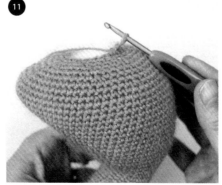

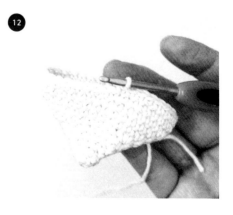

Feet and legs

Make 2, start in **Pale Pink** yarn with a 3mm (US C/2 or D/3) hook.

Round 1: 6sc in a magic ring. [6]

Round 2: Sc in all 6 sts. [6]

Round 3: (1sc, 3sc in next st, 1sc) 2 times. [10]

Round 4: (2sc, 3sc in next st, 2sc) 2 times. [14]

Round 5: Sc in all 14 sts. [14]

Round 6: (3sc, 5sc in next st, 3sc) 2 times. [22]

Round 7: (5sc, 3sc in next st, 5sc) 2 times. [26]

Round 8: (6sc, 3sc in next st, 6sc) 2 times. [30]

Round 9: (7sc, 3sc in next st, 7sc) 2 times. [34]

Rounds 10–11: Sc in all 34 sts [2 rounds] (photo 12)

Round 12: (7sc, sc3tog, 7sc) 2 times. [30]

Round 13: (6sc, sc3tog, 6sc) 2 times. [26]

Round 14: (5sc, sc3tog, 5sc) 2 times. [22]

Round 15: (4sc, sc3tog, 4sc) 2 times. [18]

Round 16: (3sc, sc3tog, 3sc) 2 times. [14]

Round 17: 3sc in next st, 4sc, 5slst, 4sc. [16]

Round 18: 1sc, 3sc in next st, 14sc. [18]

Round 19: 7sc, sc3tog, 4sc, sc3tog, 1sc. [14]

Round 20: 1sc, sc3tog, 10sc. [12] (photo 13)

Round 21: Sc in all 12 sts. [12]

Round 22: Sc3tog, 9sc. [10]

Round 23: Sc in all 10 sts. [10]

Round 24: Inv dec, 8sc. [9]

Rounds 25–36: Sc in all 9 sts. [12 rounds]

Round 37: 6sc, 3sc in next st, 2sc. [11]

Round 38: 7sc, 3sc in next st, 3sc. [13]

Round 39: 8sc, 3sc in next st, 4sc. [15]

Round 40: Sc in all 15 sts. [15]

Round 41: (inv dec, 3sc) 3 times. [12]

Round 42: (inv dec, 2sc) 3 times. [9]

Rounds 43–54: Sc in all 9 sts. [12 rounds]

Fasten off, leaving a tail for sewing. (photos 14 and 15)

Cut a piece of garden wire long enough to go into both legs and through the body, plus about 10cm (4in) extra. (photo 16)

Push the wire through the base of the body, roughly between **Rounds 63 and 64**. (photo 17)

Fold the tip of the wire down, then fold it again to create a loop shape for the foot. (photo 18)

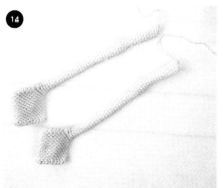

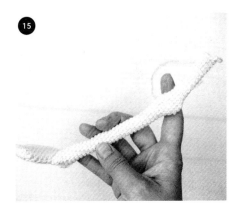

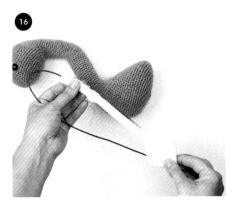

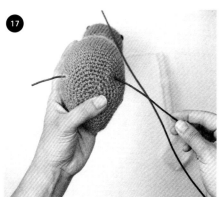

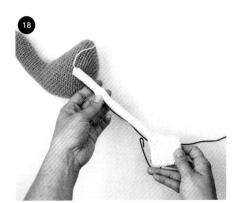

Flatten the loop down and feed it into the leg, then carefully open up the loop again inside the foot base. Repeat for the other leg. **(photos 19 and 20)**

Sew the top edge of the legs to the body, making sure that the feet face forwards. **(photo 21)**

Pinch the centre of each foot to form a ridge and sew it into place with running stitch. **(photo 22)**

Stuff the beak and sew it to the head, between the eyes. **(photo 23)**

BODy feathers

Make 1 in **Pink Mohair** yarn with a 3.5mm (US E/4) hook.

Row 1: Ch1, (ch17, start 2nd ch from hook, 4sc, 4hdc, 4dc, 4tr) 45 times, ch1. [45 feathers]

Fasten off, leaving a long tail for sewing. **(photos 24 and 25)**

The feathers will curl a little; to flatten them out soak them in warm water and then dry them flat to block.

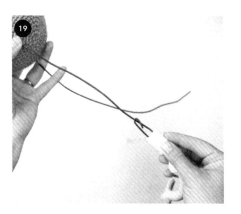

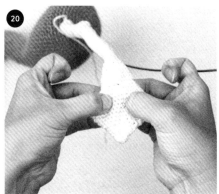

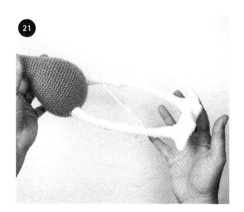

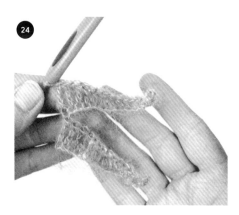

Right wing feathers

Make 1 in **Bright Pink** yarn held together with **Pink Mohair**, with a 3.5mm (US E/4) hook.

Row 1: Ch9, start 2nd ch from hook, 4sc, 4hdc, ch13, start 2nd ch from hook, 4sc, 4hdc, 4dc, ch17, start 2nd ch from hook, 4sc, 4hdc, 4dc, 4tr, ch1. [3 feathers]

Fasten off, leaving a tail for sewing.

Left wing feathers

Make 1 in **Bright Pink** yarn held together with **Pink Mohair**, with a 3.5mm (US E/4) hook.

Row 1: Ch17, start 2nd ch from hook, 4sc, 4hdc, 4dc, 4tr, ch13, start 2nd ch from hook, 4sc, 4hdc, 4dc, ch9, start 2nd ch from hook, 4sc, 4hdc, ch1. [3 feathers]

Fasten off, leaving a tail for sewing. **(photo 26)**

Once the body feathers are dry, pin them over the top of the body, arranging them in a zigzag pattern. Sew them into place with a matching sewing thread or lace weight mohair yarn. **(photos 27, 28 and 29)**

Sew the wing feathers along the side of the body, with the longest feather towards the front. **(photo 30)**

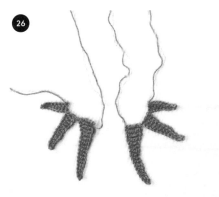

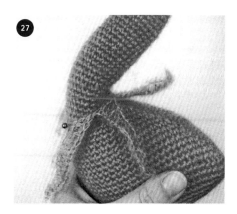

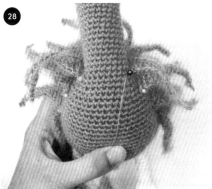

HOOPoe

The hoopoe is a rather stylish bird, with a ruffled crown of feathers and striking black and white wings, it looks full of attitude! To defend their territory, they puff up their crests to make themselves big and will use their long, sharp beaks to ward off intruders. Even the little chicks can stick up for themselves, hissing like snakes if someone comes near the nest (let's not mention their other less savoury means of self-defence...). Researchers discovered hoopoes love listening to music, bobbing their heads to the beat – just imagine a bunch of these rockers at a concert!

Dimensions

30cm (12in) tall

Yarns

Paintbox Yarns Cotton DK (100% cotton) 125m (137yds) per 50g (1¾oz) ball:

- **Orange:** 1 x 50g (1¾oz) ball in Melon Sorbet (shade 417)
- **Black:** 1 x 50g (1¾oz) ball in Pure Black (shade 402)
- **White:** 1 x 50g (1¾oz) ball in Champagne White (shade 403)

Hooks

3mm (US C/2 or D/3) hook

Other tools and materials

- Pair 10.5mm black safety eyes
- Craft wire for the legs (optional)
- Toy stuffing
- Sewing pins
- Tapestry needle

FUN FACT

Hoopoes' wing movements in flight resemble those of a butterfly. When courting, the male hoopoe brings tasty gifts to impress the female.

Tension (gauge)

Tension is not critical for this project, but if you want to match the pattern shown here, make a small circular swatch using the chosen yarn and hook (see Tools and materials: Tension swatch for the swatch pattern).

When made in DK weight cotton with a 3mm (US C/2 or D/3) hook the swatch should measure 3.5cm (1⅜in) across.

Project notes

The body of the hoopoe is worked in one piece and shaped with decreases, with the tail worked from the body at the end. Decorative feathers and wings are sewn on.

Special stitches

Front loop only (FLO): Insert the hook under the front loop only (see Crochet techniques: Front loops/back loops).

Body

Make 1 in **Orange** yarn.

Round 1: 6sc in a magic ring. [6]

Round 2: Inc in all 6 sts. [12]

Round 3: (1sc, inc in next st) 6 times. [18]

Round 4: (2sc, inc in next st) 6 times. [24]

Round 5: (3sc, inc in next st) 6 times. [30]

Round 6: (4sc, inc in next st) 6 times. [36]

Round 7: (5sc, inc in next st) 6 times. [42]

Round 8: (6sc, inc in next st) 6 times. [48]

Rounds 9–18: Sc in all 48 sts. [10 rounds]

Round 19: Inv dec, 8sc, inv dec, 36sc. [46]

Round 20: Inv dec, 6sc, inv dec, 36sc. [44]

Round 21: Inv dec, 4sc, inv dec, 36sc. [42]

Round 22: Inv dec, 2sc, inv dec, 36sc. [40]

Round 23: Inv dec 2 times, 36sc. [38]

Round 24: Inv dec, 36sc. [37]

Round 25: Inv dec, 35sc. [36] **(photo 1)**

Round 26: Sc in all 36 sts. [36]

Round 27: (inc in next st, 11sc) 3 times. [39]

Round 28: (12sc, inc in next st) 3 times. [42]

Round 29: (inc in next st, 13sc) 3 times. [45]

Round 30: (14sc, inc in next st) 3 times. [48]

Round 31: (inc in next st, 15sc) 3 times. [51]

Rounds 32–39: Sc in all 51 sts. [8 rounds]

Add the safety eyes between **Rounds 13 and 14**, either side of the decrease lines, approximately 16 stitches apart. **(photos 2 and 3)**

Round 40: (inv dec, 3sc) 3 times, 36sc. [48]

Round 41: (inv dec, 2sc) 3 times, 36sc. [45]

Round 42: (inv dec, 1sc) 3 times, 36sc. [42]

Round 43: Inv dec 3 times, 36sc. [39]

Round 44: Sc3tog, 15sc, ch2, skip 6sts, 15sc. [33] **(photo 4)**

1

2

Add toy stuffing and top up stuffing as needed.

Round 45: (inv dec, 9sc) 3 times. [30]

Round 46: (inv dec, 3sc) 6 times. [24]

Round 47: (inv dec, 2sc) 6 times. [18]

Round 48: Inv dec 9 times. [9]

Fasten off, leaving a tail. Thread tail through front loops with a tapestry needle and pull tight to close.

crest feathers

Make 6, start in **Black** yarn.

Round 1: 6sc in a magic ring. [6]

Round 2: (inc in next st, 2sc) 2 times. [8]

Round 3: Sc in all 8 sts. [8]

Rounds 4–5: Change to **White**, sc in all 8 sts. [2 rounds]

Rounds 6–13: Change to **Orange**, sc in all 8 sts. [8 rounds]

Fasten off, leaving a tail for sewing. **(photo 5)**

wings

Make 2, start in **Orange** yarn.

Round 1: 5sc in a magic ring. [5]

Round 2: Inc in all 5 sts. [10]

Round 3: (1sc, inc in next st) 5 times. [15]

Round 4: (2sc, inc in next st) 5 times. [20]

Round 5: (3sc, inc in next st) 5 times. [25]

Round 6: (4sc, inc in next st) 5 times. [30]

Round 7: Sc in all 30 sts. [30]

Round 8: Change to **Black**, sc in all 30 sts. [30]

Round 9: (inv dec, 8sc) 3 times. [27]

Round 10: Change to **White**, sc in all 27 sts. [27] **(photo 6)**

Round 11: (inv dec, 7sc) 3 times. [24]

Round 12: Change to black, sc in all 24 sts. [24]

Round 13: (inv dec, 6sc) 3 times. [21]

Round 14: Change to **White**, sc in all 21 sts. [21]

Round 15: (inv dec, 5sc) 3 times. [18]

Round 16: Change to **Black**, sc in all 18 sts. [18]

Round 17: (inv dec, 4sc) 3 times. [15]

Round 18: Change to **White**, sc in all 15 sts. [15]

Round 19: (inv dec, 3sc) 3 times. [12]

Round 20: Change to **Black**, sc in all 12 sts. [12]

Round 21: (inv dec, 2sc) 3 times. [9]

Round 22: Change to **White**, sc in all 9 sts. [9]

Round 23: (inv dec, 1sc) 3 times. [6]

Round 24: Change to **Black**, sc in all 6 sts. [6]

Fasten off, leaving a tail. Thread tail through front loops with a tapestry needle and pull tight to close. **(photo 7)**

Tail

Make 1, start in **Black** yarn. Join yarn to the first of skipped 6sts from **Round 44** of the body. **(photo 8)**

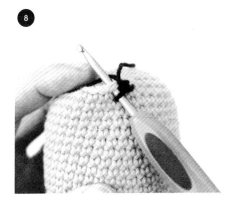

Round 1: 6sc along skipped sts, 1sc in side of gap, 2sc along the other side of the ch2, 1sc in side of gap. [10]

Round 2: Sc in all 10 sts. [10]

Rounds 3–4: Change to **White**, sc in all 10 sts. [2 rounds]

Rounds 5–6: Change to **Black**, sc in all 10 sts. [2 rounds]

Round 7: Change to **White**, 2sc, inv dec, 6sc. [9]

Round 8: Sc in all 9 sts. [9]

Round 9: Change to **Black**, 2sc, inv dec, 5sc. [8]

Round 10: Sc in all 8 sts. [8]

Fasten off, fold the tip flat and sew the end closed. **(photo 9)**

Feet

Make 2, start in **Black** yarn.

Round 1: 6sc in a magic ring. [6]

In the next round we make the toes.

Round 2: Working in FLO, (slst in next st, ch5, start 2nd ch from hook, 4sc along the ch, slst in same st) 3 times, slst in next 2sts, ch3, start 2nd ch from hook, 2slst along the ch, slst in same st, slst in next st. [4 toes] **(photo 10)**

Round 3: Working in back loops from Round 1, sc in all 6 sts. [6] **(photo 11)**

Rounds 4–8: Sc in all 6 sts. [5 rounds]

Round 9: Change to **Orange**, inc in all 6 sts. [12]

Round 10: Sc in all 12 sts. [12]

Fasten off, leaving a tail for sewing. **(photo 12)**

Beak

Make 1 in **Black** yarn.

Round 1: 5sc in a magic ring. [5]

Rounds 2–3: Sc in all 5 sts. [2 rounds]

Round 4: Inc in next st, 4sc. [6]

Rounds 5–6: Sc in all 6 sts. [2 rounds]

Round 7: Inc in next st, 5sc. [7]

Rounds 8–9: Sc in all 7 sts. [2 rounds]

Round 10: Inc in next st, 6sc. [8]

Rounds 11–12: Sc in all 8 sts. [2 rounds]

Round 13: Inc in next st, 7sc. [9]

Round 14: Sc in all 9 sts. [9]

Fasten off, leaving a tail for sewing.

Sew the beak to the front of the head between the eyes. **(photo 13)**

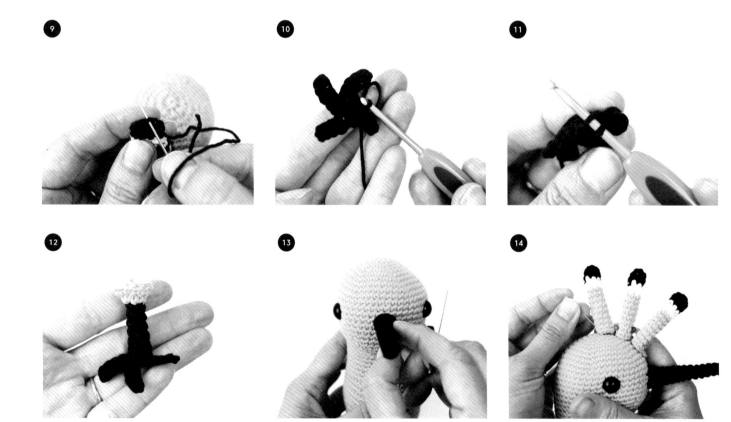

Final details

Pin the crest feathers over the top of the head like a mohican and then sew them into place. **(photos 14 and 15)**

Sew the wings to the sides of the body. **(photos 16 and 17)**

Sew the feet to the bottom of the body between **Rounds 41 and 45**, inserting wire into them if you wish (see Flamingo: Feet and legs). **(photos 18, 19 and 20)**

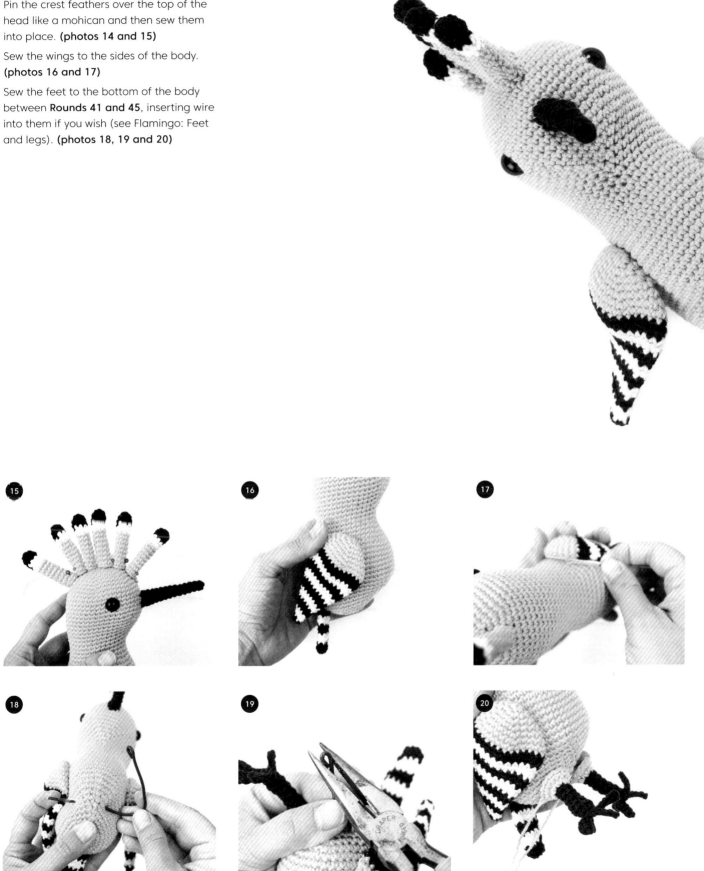

Chameleon

With beautiful jewel-like scales, a grumpy expression and those famously long tongues, chameleons are charismatic reptiles. It's fascinating to watch them walk gingerly along a branch and to see their eyes lock onto their prey. Their behaviour looks more like a funky dance than the hunt of an experienced predator! Chameleons are known for their colour-changing ability; however, it seems this neat trick is designed not to help them blend in with their background but to adjust body temperature and express their emotions – the brighter the colours the feistier they feel!

Dimensions

23cm (9in) long in 4-ply cotton held double or 16cm (6¼in) long if made in DK weight cotton

Yarns

Paintbox Yarns Cotton 4-ply (100% cotton), 170m (186yds) per 50g (1¾oz) ball held double:

- **Teal:** 1 x 50g (1¾oz) ball in Sea Green (shade 21)
- **Mint:** 1 x 50g (1¾oz) ball in Mint Green (shade 16)

Alternatively, you could make the chameleon in a speckled or variegated yarn

Hooks

3mm (US C/2 or D/3) hook

3.5mm (US E/4) hook

Other tools and materials

- Pair 12mm black safety eyes
- Craft pipe cleaners (chenille stems) or wire (optional)
- Toy stuffing
- Sewing pins
- Tapestry needle

FUN FACT

Over half of all known chameleon species live on the island of Madagascar and the smallest chameleon is the same size as a matchstick head!

Tension (gauge)

Tension is not critical for this project, but if you want to match the pattern shown here, make a small circular swatch using the chosen yarn and hook (see Tools and materials: Tension swatch for the swatch pattern).

When made with two strands of 4-ply weight cotton HELD DOUBLE with a 3.5mm (US E/4) hook the swatch should measure 4cm (1⅝in) across. When made with a single strand of 4-ply weight cotton with a 3mm (US C/2 or D/3) hook the swatch should measure 3cm (1¼in) across.

Project notes

The chameleon's body is worked in one piece, starting at the nose. Holding the two yarns together creates a speckled look all over. You could try using scraps of different tones of the same yarn to get an even more varied texture. The legs are worked from the body and can be reinforced with wire. The toy is finished with crab stitch details.

Special stitches

Crab stitch (reverse single crochet): Working from the left to the right, insert hook into next st, yarn over, pull through to the front of the work, yarn over, pull through the 2 loops on the hook.

Eyes

Make 2 in **Teal** yarn held double, with a 3.5mm (US E/4) hook.

Ch6, slst into 1st st to make a ring.

Round 1: 8sc into the ring. [8]

Rounds 2–3: Sc in all 8 sts. [2 rounds]

Round 4: (1sc, inc in next st) 4 times. [12]

Round 5: (inc in next st, 2sc) 4 times. [16]

Round 6: Sc in all 16 sts. [16]

Fasten off, leaving a tail for sewing. **(photo 1)**

Push the centre inwards and place a safety eye through the middle of each piece, but don't fasten them yet. **(photo 2)**

Head, body and tail

Make 1 in **Teal** and **Mint** yarns held together with a 3.5mm (US E/4) hook.

Ch9, start 2nd ch from hook, work on both sides of the chain.

Round 1: 8sc along the top of the chain, turn over and work back to the start, 8sc along the other side of the chain. [16] **(photo 3)**

Round 2: (inc in next st, 6sc, inc in next st) 2 times. [20]

Round 3: (1sc, inc in next st, 6sc, inc in next st, 1sc) 2 times. [24]

Round 4: Sc in all 24 sts. [24]

Round 5: 2sc, 8slst, 14sc. [24]

Round 6: 3sc, inc 3 times, 2sc, inc 3 times, 13sc. [30]

Round 7: 3sc, (1sc, inc in next st) 3 times, 2sc, (inc in next st, 1sc) 3 times, 13sc. [36]

Round 8: 6sc, (2sc, inc in next st) 4 times, 18sc. [40]

Round 9: 9sc, inc in next st, 10sc, inc in next st, 19sc. [42] **(photo 4)**

Rounds 10–15: Sc in all 42 sts. [6 rounds]

Round 16: 18sc, 3sc in next st, 23sc. [44]

Round 17: 19sc, 3sc in next st, 24sc. [46]

Round 18: 20sc, 3sc in next st, 25sc. [48]

Round 19: 21sc, 3sc in next st, 26sc. [50]

Round 20: 1sc, inv dec 3 times, 15sc, 3sc in next st, 15sc, inv dec 3 times, 6sc. [46]

Round 21: 4slst, 33sc, 9slst. [46] **(photo 5)**

Round 22: 17sc, inv dec, inv sc3tog, inv dec, 22sc. [42]

Round 23: 15sc, inv dec, inv sc3tog, inv dec, 20sc. [38]

Round 24: 13sc, inv dec, inv sc3tog, inv dec, 18sc. [34]

Add the safety eyes and eye pieces between **Rounds 13 and 14**, towards the lower edge of the head. Secure the backs of the safety eyes. **(photo 6)**

The next round marks the position of the front legs.

Round 25: 3sc, 3sc in next st, 8sc, 5slst, 8sc, 3sc in next st, 8sc. [38]

Round 26: 4sc, 3sc in next st, 12sc, inc in next st, 10sc, 3sc in next st, 9sc. [43]

Round 27: 3sc, skip 5sts, ch1, 22sc, skip 5sts, ch1, 8sc. [35] **(photo 7)**

Rounds 28–30: Sc in all 35 sts. [3 rounds]

Round 31: 16sc, inv dec, 17sc. [34]

Round 32: 16sc, inv dec, 16sc. [33]

Round 33: 15sc, inv dec, 16sc. [32]

The next round marks the position of the back legs.

Round 34: 4sc, skip 1st, ch5, 10sc, inv dec, 9sc, skip 1st, ch5, 4sc. [38] **(photo 8)**

Round 35: 5sc, sc3tog, 10sc, inv dec, 10sc, sc3tog, 6sc. [34]

Round 36: 3sc, inv dec 3 times, 7sc, inv dec, 7sc, inv dec 3 times, 3sc. [27]

Round 37: 11sc, inv dec 2 times, 11sc, inc in next st. [26]

Round 38: 10sc, inv dec 2 times, 12sc. [24]

Add toy stuffing, filling out the nose and crest. Add more stuffing as you go.

Round 39: 3slst, 8sc, inv dec, 8sc, 3slst. [23]

Round 40: 10sc, inv dec, 11sc. [22]

Round 41: 3slst, 7sc, inv dec, 7sc, 3slst. [21]

Round 42: 9sc, inv dec, 10sc. [20] **(photo 9)**

Round 43: 9sc, inv dec, 9sc. [19]

Round 44: 8sc, inv sc3tog, 8sc. [17]

Round 45: 7sc, inv sc3tog, 7sc. [15]

Rounds 46–47: Sc in all 15 sts. [2 rounds]

Round 48: 6sc, inv sc3tog, 6sc. [13]

Rounds 49–50: Sc in all 13 sts. [2 rounds]

Fasten off **Mint** and continue with two strands of **Teal**, using the strand from inside the ball as the second.

Round 51: 5sc, inv sc3tog, 5sc. [11]

Rounds 52–53: Sc in all 11 sts. [2 rounds]

Round 54: 4sc, sc3tog, 4sc. [9]

Rounds 55–56: Sc in all 9 sts. [2 rounds]

Round 57: 3sc, sc3tog, 3sc. [7]

Rounds 58–59: Sc in all 7 sts. [2 rounds]

Drop one strand of **Teal** and change to a 3mm (US C/2 or D/3) hook.

Rounds 60–72: Sc in all 7 sts. [13 rounds]

Add extra rounds here if you want a longer tail!

Fasten off, leaving a tail. Insert a long craft pipe cleaner (chenille stem) or wire into the chameleon's tail. Thread yarn tail through front loops with a tapestry needle and pull tight to close. Roll up the end of the tail. **(photo 10)**

Stitch down the outer edge of the eyes. **(photo 11)**

Legs

Make 4 in **Teal** yarn held double with a 3.5mm (US E/4) hook.

For the front legs, join the yarn to the first of the skipped stitches. For the back legs, join the yarn to the first of the new chains.

Round 1: 5sc along the skipped stitches/chains, 1sc into the side of the gap, 1sc into the stitch/chain on next row, 1sc into the other side of the gap. [8] **(photo 12)**

Rounds 2–4: Sc in all 8 sts. [3 rounds]

Round 5: Inv dec 2 times, 4sc. [6]

Round 6: 2slst, 1sc, inc 2 times, 1sc. [8]

Round 7: 2slst, 6sc. [8]

Rounds 8–13: Sc in all 8 sts. [6 rounds]

Round 14: (inv dec, 2sc) 2 times. [6]

Round 15: Sc in all 6 sts. [6]

Round 16: (1sc, 3sc in next st, 1sc) 2 times. [10]

Round 17: (1slst, 1sc, 3sc in next st, 1sc, 1slst) 2 times. [14]

Fasten off, leaving a tail for sewing. **(photo 13)**

Soles

Make 4 in **Mint** yarn held double with a 3.5mm (US E/4) hook.

Round 1: 6sc in a magic ring. [6]

Round 2: (1sc, 3sc in next st, 1sc) 2 times. [10]

Round 3: (1slst, 1sc, 3sc in next st, 1sc, 1slst) 2 times. [14]

Fasten off and weave in the ends. **(photo 14)**

Jaw

Make 1 in **Mint** yarn held double with a 3.5mm (US E/4) hook.

Ch9, start 2nd ch from hook, work on both sides of the chain.

Round 1: 8sc along the top of the chain, turn over and work back to the start, 8sc along the other side of the chain. [16]

Round 2: (inc in next st, 6sc, inc in next st) 2 times. [20]

Round 3: (1sc, inc in next st, 6sc, inc in next st, 1sc) 2 times. [24]

Round 4: 2sc, 3sc in next st, 9sc, inc in next st, 9sc, 3sc in next st, 1sc. [29]

Round 5: 3slst, 3sc in next st, 22sc, 3sc in next st, 2slst. [33]

Fasten off, leaving a tail for sewing. **(photo 15)**

Final details

At this point you can insert some wire into the legs if you want them to be poseable. You could twist two craft pipe cleaners (chenille stems) together, shaping the tips into toes on one side, then feed the rest through a bendy straw – the straw is easier to push through the first leg and out the other side. Twist the tips on the other end and trim off any extra wire. **(photos 16 and 17)**

Place a sole over the base of each leg and sew them into place. **(photo 18)**

Secure the crest into a flatter shape with a short stitch near its base using some **Teal** yarn. This brings the front and back a little closer together. **(photo 19)**

Add a row of crab stitch down the spine to decorate. **(photo 20)**

Sew the jaw to the base of the head, catching the shape just under the top loops when going around the outer edge – this will give a neat line to the mouth edge. **(photo 21)**

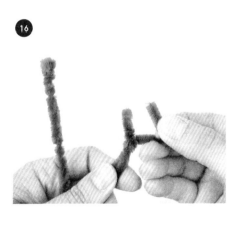

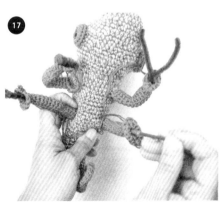

CROCODILE

Crocodiles have been around for more than 200 million years, with some mighty species growing as large as six metres (20 feet) long. Famously, crocodiles stay perfectly still in the murky water waiting for the opportune moment to snap their toothy jaws on their prey. Some even go the extra mile and use sticks and twigs to lure birds into landing on their snouts – then snap them up for a nice snack. Other species can take on sharks and climb trees ... wow! I wouldn't want to get too close to this apex predator, except in cuddly toy form, of course!

Dimensions

50cm (20in) long

Yarns

Paintbox Yarns Cotton DK (100% cotton), 125m (137yds) per 50g (1¾oz) ball:

- **Green:** 3 x 50g (1¾oz) balls in Racing Green (shade 428)
- **Lime:** 1 x 50g (1¾oz) ball in Lime Green (shade 429)
- **Red:** 1 x 50g (1¾oz) ball in Red Wine (shade 416)
- **White:** 1 x 50g (1¾oz) ball in Champagne White (shade 403)
- **Yellow:** 1 x 50g (1¾oz) ball in Daffodil Yellow (shade 422)

Hooks

2.5mm (US B/1) hook

3mm (US C/2 or D/3) hook

Other tools and materials

- Pair 8mm black safety eyes
- Toy stuffing
- Thick felt or fabric stabilizer
- Sewing pins
- Tapestry needle

FUN FACT

If a crocodile loses a tooth, there's always another one ready to fill the gap. In fact, crocodiles can go through thousands of teeth in their lifetime!

Tension (gauge)

Tension is not critical for this project, but if you want to match the pattern shown here, make a small circular swatch using the chosen yarn and hook (see Tools and materials: Tension swatch for the swatch pattern).

When made in DK weight cotton with a 3mm (US C/2 or D/3) hook the swatch should measure 3.5cm (1⅜in) across.

Project notes

The crocodile's body is made in one piece, starting at the tip of the tail. The jaws are split into two sections with a chain and are worked separately. A red oval inner mouth completes the body. Decorative spikes and teeth are sewn on at the end.

Body

Make 1 in **Green** yarn with a 3mm (US C/2 or D/3) hook.

Round 1: 6sc in a magic ring. [6]

Round 2: Sc in all 6 sts. [6]

Round 3: (inc in next st, 2sc) 2 times. [8]

Round 4: (inc in next st, 3sc) 2 times. [10]

Round 5: (inc in next st, 4sc) 2 times. [12]

Round 6: (inc in next st, 5sc) 2 times. [14]

Round 7: (inc in next st, 6sc) 2 times. [16]

Round 8: (inc in next st, 7sc) 2 times. [18]

Round 9: (inc in next st, 8sc) 2 times. [20]

Round 10: (inc in next st, 9sc) 2 times. [22]

Round 11: (inc in next st, 10sc) 2 times. [24]

Round 12: (inc in next st, 11sc) 2 times. [26]

Round 13: (inc in next st, 12sc) 2 times. [28]

Round 14: (inc in next st, 13sc) 2 times. [30]

Round 15: (inc in next st, 14sc) 2 times. [32]

Round 16: (inc in next st, 15sc) 2 times. [34]

Round 17: Sc in all 34 sts. [34]

Round 18: (inc in next st, 16sc) 2 times. [36]

Round 19: Sc in all 36 sts. [36]

Round 20: (inc in next st, 17sc) 2 times. [38]

Round 21: Sc in all 38 sts. [38]

Round 22: (inc in next st, 18sc) 2 times. [40]

Round 23: Sc in all 40 sts. [40]

Round 24: (inc in next st, 19sc) 2 times. [42]

Rounds 25–26: Sc in all 42 sts. [2 rounds]

Round 27: (inc in next st, 20sc) 2 times. [44]

Rounds 28–29: Sc in all 44 sts. [2 rounds]

Round 30: (inc in next st, 21sc) 2 times. [46]

Rounds 31–32: Sc in all 46 sts. [2 rounds]

Round 33: (inc in next st, 22sc) 2 times. [48]

Rounds 34–35: Sc in all 48 sts. [2 rounds]

Round 36: (inc in next st, 23sc) 2 times. [50]

Rounds 37–46: Sc in all 50 sts. [10 rounds]

Round 47: (inv dec, 8sc) 5 times. [45]

Round 48: (inv dec, 7sc) 5 times. [40] **(photo 1)**

Round 49: Sc in all 40 sts. [40]

The next section is the body.

Round 50: (inc in next st, 3sc) 10 times. [50]

Round 51: (2sc, inc in next st, 2sc) 10 times. [60]

Rounds 52–84: Sc in all 60 sts. [33 rounds]

Round 85: (inv dec 5 times, 20sc) 2 times. [50]

Round 86: Sc in all 50 sts. [50]

In the next section the head is shaped.

Round 87: 5sc, (inc in next st, 1sc) 10 times, 25sc. [60]

Round 88: Inc 5 times, 30sc, inc 5 times, 20sc. [70]

Rounds 89–93: Sc in all 70 sts. [5 rounds] **(photo 2)**

In the next round, increases to mark the positions of the eyes are started.

Round 94: 15sc, 3sc in next st, 18sc, 3sc in next st, 35sc. [74]

Round 95: 16sc, 3sc in next st, 20sc, 3sc in next st, 36sc. [78]

Round 96: 17sc, inc in next st, 22sc, inc in next st, 37sc. [80]

Rounds 97–98: Sc in all 80 sts. [2 rounds]

Round 99: 13sc, inv dec, 7sc, inv dec, 12sc, inv dec, 7sc, inv dec, 33sc. [76]

Round 100: 12sc, inv dec, 7sc, inv dec, 10sc, inv dec, 7sc, inv dec, 32sc. [72]

Round 101: (14sc, inv dec, 1sc, inv dec) 2 times, 34sc. [68] **(photo 3)**

Round 102: 13sc, inv dec, 1sc, inv dec, 12sc, inv dec, 1sc, inv dec, 33sc. [64]

Round 103: 12sc, inv dec, 1sc, inv dec, 10sc, inv dec, 1sc, inv dec, 32sc. [60]

The next round splits the head into the upper and lower jaws.

Round 104: 36sc, ch24, skip 24sts to end of the round and 4sts from the beginning of next round. [60] **(photo 4)**

Round 105: 32sc along the main round, 24sc along the chain. [56]

Round 106: 32sc, inv dec, 20sc, inv dec. [54]

Round 107: 32sc, inv dec, 18sc, inv dec. [52]

Round 108: 32sc, inv dec, 16sc, inv dec. [50]

Rounds 109–120: Sc in all 50 sts. [12 rounds]

Round 121: 2sc, inv dec, 32sc, inv dec, 12sc. [48]

Rounds 122–123: Sc in all 48 sts. [2 rounds]

Round 124: 2sc, inv dec, 31sc, inv dec, 11sc. [46]

Rounds 125–126: Sc in all 46 sts. [2 rounds]

Round 127: 1sc, inv dec, 31sc, inv dec, 10sc. [44]

Rounds 128–129: Sc in all 44 sts. [2 rounds]

Round 130: 1sc, inv dec, 30sc, inv dec, 9sc. [42]

Rounds 131–132: Sc in all 42 sts. [2 rounds]

Round 133: (5sc, inv dec) 6 times. [36]

Round 134: (2sc, inv dec, 2sc) 6 times. [30]

Round 135: (inv dec, 3sc) 6 times. [24]

Round 136: (2sc, inv dec) 6 times. [18]

Round 137: (inv dec, 1sc) 6 times. [12]

Round 138: Inv dec 6 times. [6]

Fasten off, leaving a tail. Thread tail through front loops with a tapestry needle and pull tight to close. **(photo 5)**

Bottom Jaw

Make 1 in **Green** yarn with a 3mm (US C/2 or D/3) hook.

Round 1: Join yarn to the first of skipped stitches from **Round 104** of body, 28sc, ch20. [48] **(photos 6 and 7)**

Round 2: 28sc, 20sc along the ch. [48]

Round 3: Sc in all 48 sts. [48]

Round 4: 28sc, inv dec, 16sc, inv dec. [46]

Rounds 5–16: Sc in all 46 sts. [12 rounds]

Round 17: Inv dec, 28sc, inv dec, 14sc. [44]

Rounds 18–21: Sc in all 44 sts. [4 rounds]

Round 22: Inv dec, 27sc, inv dec, 13sc. [42]

Rounds 23–24: Sc in all 42 sts. [2 rounds]

Round 25: (5sc, inv dec) 6 times. [36]

Round 26: (2sc, inv dec, 2sc) 6 times. [30]

Round 27: (inv dec, 3sc) 6 times. [24]

Round 28: (2sc inv dec) 6 times. [18]

Round 29: (inv dec, 1sc) 6 times. [12]

Round 30: Inv dec 6 times. [6]

Fasten off, leaving a tail. Thread tail through front loops with a tapestry needle and pull tight to close. **(photo 8)**

Using the thick felt or stabilizer, cut out two shapes matching the size and shape of the jaws. Place them inside the jaws. **(photos 9 and 10)**

Add toy stuffing to the body and jaws.

Mouth

Make 1 in **Red** yarn with a 3mm (US C/2 or D/3) hook.

Ch37, start 2nd ch from hook.

Round 1: 36sc along top of chain, turn work, 36sc along other side of the chain. [72]

Round 2: (inc in next st, 34sc, inc in next st) 2 times. [76]

Round 3: (1sc, inc in next st, 34sc, inc in next st, 1sc) 2 times. [80]

Round 4: (inc in next st, 1sc, inc in next st, 34sc, inc in next st, 1sc, inc in next st) 2 times. [88]

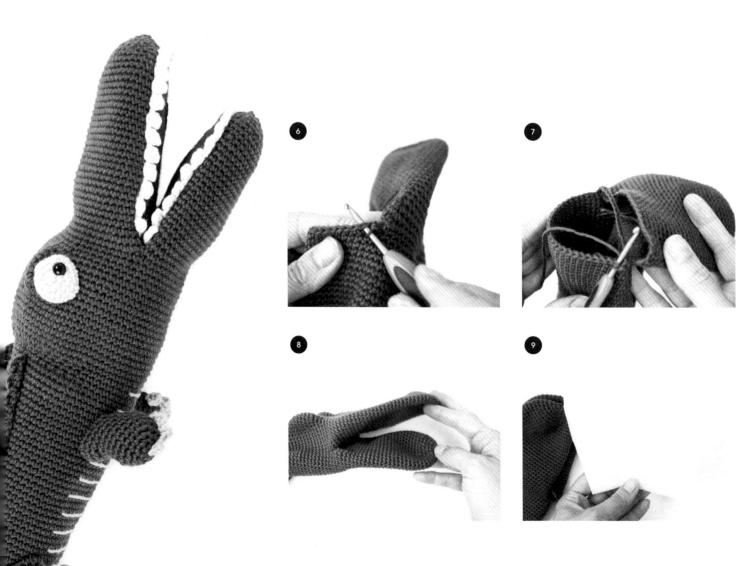

Round 5: (2sc, inc in next st, 38sc, inc in next st, 2sc) 2 times. [92]

Round 6: [(1sc, inc in next st) 3 times, 34sc, (inc in next st, 1sc) 3 times] 2 times. [104]

Round 7: (6sc, inc in next st, 38sc, inc in next st, 6sc) 2 times. [108]

Round 8: [(2sc, inc in next st) 3 times, 36sc, (inc in next st, 2sc) 3 times] 2 times. [120]

Round 9: Sc in all 120 sts. [120]

Fasten off **Red**, leaving a long tail for sewing. **(photo 11)**

Pin the mouth into the jaws and sew it into place. The top should sit lightly forward of the bottom. **(photo 12)**

Teeth, claws and back spikes

The spikes are all worked in the same way. Use a smaller hook size for the teeth spikes.

Row 1: (ch3, 1dc in 2nd ch from hook, 1hdc in next ch) repeat the number of times needed.

For the teeth, using **White** yarn and a 2.5mm (US B/1) hook, make one strip with 27 spikes for the upper jaw and one strip with 22 spikes for lower jaw. **(photo 13)**

For the claws, using **Lime** yarn and a 3mm (US C/2 or D/3) hook, make four strips with three spikes on each.

For the back spikes, using **Green** yarn and a 3mm (US C/2 or D/3) hook, make one strip with 29 spikes for the tail and spine and two strips with 12 spikes each for the sides.

Fasten off, leaving a tail for sewing. **(photo 14)**

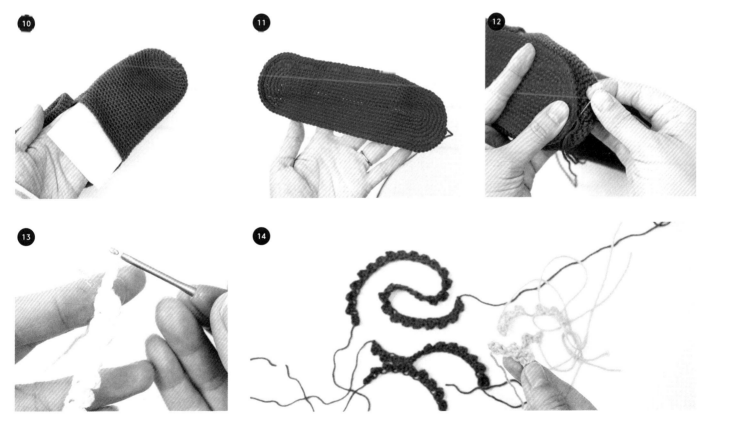

Feet

Make 4 in **Green** yarn with a 3mm (US C/2 or D/3) hook.

Round 1: 6sc in a magic ring. [6]

Round 2: (1sc, 3sc in next st, 1sc) 2 times. [10]

Round 3: (2sc, 3sc in next st, 2sc) 2 times. [14]

Round 4: (3sc, 3sc in next st, 3sc) 2 times. [18]

Rounds 5–8: Sc in all 18 sts. [4 rounds]

Round 9: 3sc, inc 3 times, 5sc, inv dec 3 times, 1sc. [18]

Round 10: 4sc, inc 3 times, 5sc, inv dec 3 times. [18]

Rounds 11–12: Sc in all 18 sts. [2 rounds]

Fasten off, leaving a tail for sewing. **(photo 15)**

Eyes

Make 2 in **Yellow** yarn with a 3mm (US C/2 or D/3) hook.

Round 1: 6sc in a magic ring. [6]

Round 2: Inc 6 times. [12]

Round 3: (1sc, inc in next st) 6 times. [18]

Rounds 4–5: Sc in all 18 sts. [2 rounds]

Fasten off, leaving a tail for sewing. **(photo 16)**

Assembly

Pin the strips of teeth along the edges of the mouth and stitch them into place catching them in-between each spike with the thread. **(photo 17)**

Pin the longest green spike strip along the centre of the back and tail and the shorter strips on either side of the centre back, then stitch into place. **(photos 18 and 19)**

Add a small amount of stuffing to the feet and sew them to the sides of the body. **(photo 20)**

Sew the claws to the tips of each foot. **(photo 21)**

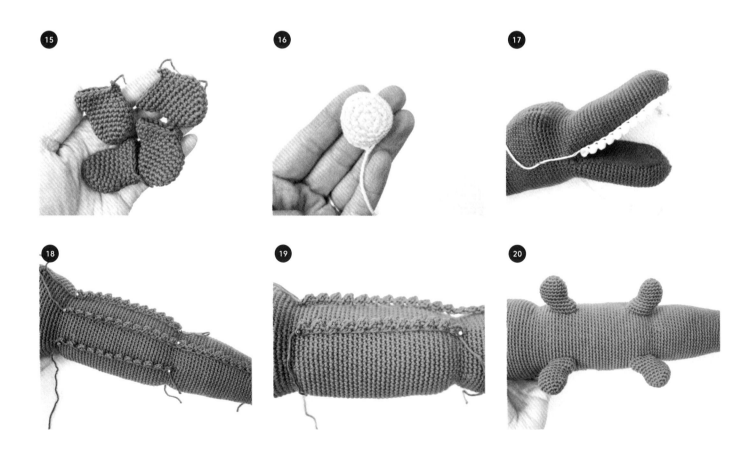

Add safety eyes to the yellow eye pieces between **Rounds 2 and 3** and then sew them to the sides of the head, with the safety eyes positioned towards the mouth. Add a bit of stuffing under the eye pieces as you sew. **(photos 22 and 23)**

If needed, at this point you could top up the head's stuffing through the gaps in the mouth corners, then sew up the corners with **Green** yarn. **(photo 24)**

Final details

Embroider some stripes onto the tail and tummy using **Lime** yarn. **(photo 25)**

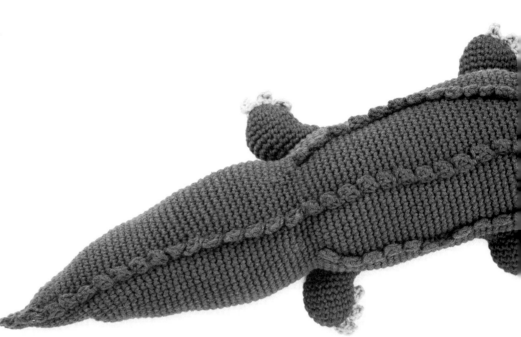

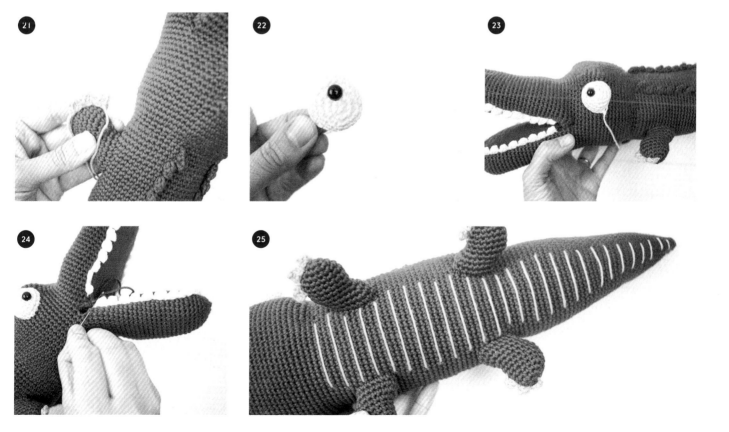

MARY RIVER TURTLE

This quirky reptile lives in the Mary River in Australia, growing its distinctive head of algae hair only in these waters. Doesn't it look like something from a fantasy film? This punky hairdo isn't the only odd thing about this species. These turtles have two ways of breathing: as well as breathing in air like we do, they can also take water into their cloaca tail opening and extract oxygen straight from the water. The longest recorded time a Mary River turtle spent under water is three whole days – very impressive indeed!

Dimensions

23cm (9in) long

Yarns

Paintbox Yarns Cotton DK (100% cotton), 125m (137yds) per 50g (1¾oz) ball:

- **Lilac:** 1 x 50g (1¾oz) ball in Pale Lilac (shade 446)
- **Purple:** 1 x 50g (1¾oz) ball in Pansy Purple (shade 448)
- **Lime:** 1 x 50g (1¾oz) ball in Lime Green (shade 429)

Scraps of other green yarns

Hooks

3mm (US C/2 or D/3) hook

Other tools and materials

- Pair 8mm black safety eyes
- Toy stuffing
- Sewing pins
- Sewing clips
- Tapestry needle

FUN FACT

Only identified as a species in 1994, the Mary River turtle is one of Australia's largest freshwater turtles. Their shells can grow to nearly 50cm (20in) long.

Tension (gauge)

Tension is not critical for this project, but, if you want to match the pattern shown here, make a small circular swatch using the chosen yarn and hook (see Tools and materials: Tension swatch for the swatch pattern).

When made in DK weight cotton with a 3mm (US C/2 or D/3) hook the swatch should measure 3.5cm (1⅜in) across.

Project notes

This project uses slip stitches to join in the individual pieces under the big shell. Decorate your turtle's shell with embroidered patterns and add as much green hair as you like!

Head

Make 1 in **Lilac** yarn.

Round 1: 6sc in a magic ring. [6]

Round 2: Sc in all 6 sts. [6]

Round 3: (1sc, inc in next st) 6 times. [18]

Rounds 4–5: Sc in all 18 sts. [2 rounds]

Round 6: 3sc in next st, 5sc, 3sc in next st, 11sc. [22]

Round 7: 1sc, 3sc in next st, 7sc, 3sc in next st, 12sc. [26]

Round 8: 2sc, 3sc in next st, 9sc, 3sc in next st, 13sc. [30] **(photo 1)**

Rounds 9–16: Sc in all 30 sts. [8 rounds]

Round 17: (2sc, inv dec) 5 times, 10sc. [25]

Round 18: (1sc, inv dec) 5 times, 10sc. [20]

Add the safety eyes between **Rounds 8 and 9**, above the decreases. Use the 10sc section from the last two rounds as a guide. **(photo 2)**

Round 19: Inv dec 5 times, 10sc. [15]

Add stuffing to the head and top up as you work.

Rounds 20–24: Sc in all 15 sts. [5 rounds]

Round 25: Fold the edge flat and work 7sc through both layers to close the edge. [7]

Fasten off. **(photo 3)**

Feet

Make 4 in **Lilac** yarn.

Round 1: 7sc in a magic ring. [7]

Round 2: Inc in all 7 sts. [14]

Round 3: (1sc, inc in next st) 7 times. [21]

Rounds 4–7: Sc in all 21 sts. [4 rounds]

Round 8: (inv dec, 5sc) 3 times. [18]

Round 9: (inv dec, 4sc) 3 times. [15]

Rounds 10–14: Sc in all 15 sts. [5 rounds]

Add a little bit of stuffing.

Round 15: Fold the edge flat and work 7sc through both layers to close the edge. [7]

Fasten off. **(photo 4)**

Tail

Make 1 in **Lilac** yarn.

Round 1: 5sc in a magic ring. [5]

Round 2: Sc in all 5 sts. [5]

Round 3: 2sc, inc in next st, 2sc. [6]

Round 4: 2sc, inc in next st, 3sc. [7]

Round 5: 3sc, inc in next st, 3sc. [8]

Round 6: 3sc, inc in next st, 4sc. [9]

Round 7: 4sc, inc in next st, 4sc. [10]

Round 8: 4sc, inc in next st, 5sc. [11]

Round 9: 5sc, inc in next st, 5sc. [12]

Round 10: 5sc, inc in next st, 6sc. [13]

Round 11: Sc in all 13 sts. [13]

Add toy stuffing.

Round 12: 3sc, fold the edge flat, work 6sc through both layers to close the end. [6]

Fasten off. **(photo 5)**

Bottom shell

Make 1 in **Purple** yarn.

Round 1: 7sc in a magic ring. [7]

Round 2: Inc in all 7 sts. [14]

Round 3: (1sc, inc in next st) 7 times. [21]

Round 4: (2sc, inc in next st) 7 times. [28]

Round 5: (3sc, inc in next st) 7 times. [35]

Round 6: (4sc, inc in next st) 7 times. [42]

Round 7: (5sc, inc in next st) 7 times. [49]

Round 8: 24sc, 3sc in next st, 24sc. [51]

Round 9: 25sc, 3sc in next st, 25sc. [53]

Round 10: 26sc, 3sc in next st, 26sc. [55]

Round 11: 27sc, 3sc in next st, 27sc. [57]

Round 12: 28sc, 3sc in next st, 28sc. [59]

Fasten off, leaving a tail. **(photo 6)**

Top shell

Make 1 in **Purple** yarn.

Round 1: 6sc in a magic ring. [6]

Round 2: Inc in all 6 sts. [12]

Round 3: (1sc, inc in next st) 6 times. [18]

Round 4: (2sc, inc in next st) 6 times. [24]

Round 5: (3sc, inc in next st) 6 times. [30]

Round 6: (4sc, inc in next st) 6 times. [36]

Round 7: (5sc, inc in next st) 6 times. [42]

Round 8: (6sc, inc in next st) 6 times. [48]

Round 9: Inc in next st, 47sc. [49]

Round 10: 24sc, 3sc in next st, 24sc. [51]

Round 11: 25sc, 3sc in next st, 25sc. [53]

Round 12: 26sc, 3sc in next st, 26sc. [55]

Round 13: 27sc, 3sc in next st, 27sc. [57]

Round 14: 28sc, 3sc in next st, 26sc, skip last 2 sts. [57 + 2 skipped sts] **(photo 7)**

Keep the yarn live and proceed to joining the shell halves and adding in the other pieces. You could clip the pieces together with sewing clips to stop them moving. **(photo 8)**

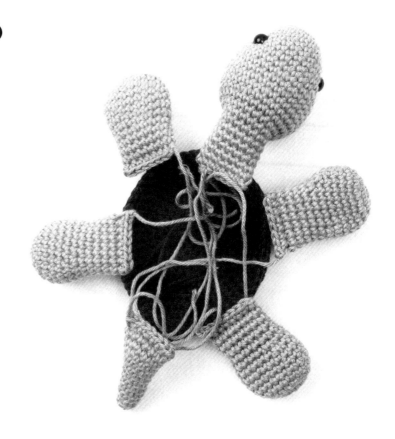

Round 15: 7slst through top shell, head and bottom shell, 2slst through the shells. Join in first foot – 7slst through all layers, 4slst through the shells. Join in next foot – 7slst through all layers, 3slst though the shells. Join in tail – 6slst through all layers, 3slst through the shells. Join in next foot – 7 slst through all layers, 4slst through the shells. Add stuffing to the shell. Join in last foot – 7slst through all layers, 2slst through the shells. [59] **(photos 9 and 10)**

Round 16: Working into the slip stitches along the top shell, 30sc, 3sc in next st, 28sc. [61] **(photo 11)**

Fasten off and weave in the ends.

chin barbels

Make 1 in **Lilac** yarn.

Row 1: (ch3, start 2nd ch from hook, 2slst) 2 times. [2 barbels]

Fasten off, leaving a tail for sewing. **(photo 12)**

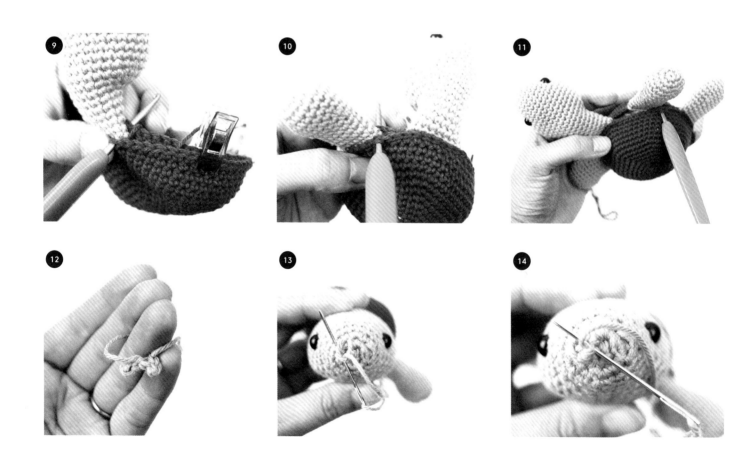

Final details

Embroider some nostrils in **Lilac** yarn: mark out two circles, then wrap yarn around each circle to raise the edges. **(photos 13 and 14)**

Cut some small strands of **Lime** yarn and any extra mohair or other textured green yarns and add them to the top of the head to make the punk haircut. **(photos 15 and 16)**

Pinch the tip of each foot and embroider them with **Purple** yarn to look like flippers. Secure the embroidered lines with a tiny claw at each end. Make the claws by overlapping a couple of short stitches over the same spot. **(photos 17 and 18)**

Sew the barbels to the front of the head and embroider a smile in **Purple** yarn. **(photo 19)**

Decorate the shell with some **Lilac** yarn embroidery and, if you like, more green tufts of hair to finish your turtle! **(photo 20)**

CROCHET TECHNIQUES

For most of the projects you will work in single crochet, increasing and decreasing stitches as needed. The samples are made in the classic v-style single crochet, but it is possible to work them as the twisted x-style single crochet instead.

Invisible decreases are used throughout the book, but feel free to use your preferred type of decrease. Likewise, most projects start with a magic ring, but this can be substituted for a ch2 start.

All the pieces are worked in a continuous spiral with no slip stitches joining the rounds at the ends. If something is crocheted in rows it will begin with 'Row' instead of 'Round'. For more information, see How to use this book: How to read the patterns.

slip knot

A slip knot is a common way to start a foundation chain, there are different ways to do it, but this is the quickest. Feel free to use your preferred way!

1. Loop the yarn around the hook with the main yarn thread on top (1).

2. With the hook, pull the main yarn thread through to make the first loop (2).

chain (ch)

1. With the slip knot loop on the hook and pinching the yarn tail between your thumb and index finger, wrap the yarn around the hook – this is a yarn over (3).

2. Pull the yarn through the loop on the hook. First chain made. Repeat as many times as needed (4).

slip stitch (slst)

Insert hook into the stitch or chain and yarn over (5). Pull a loop through the stitch and the loop on the hook to complete (6).

single crochet (sc)

Single crochet stitch is what gives amigurumi-style toys their distinctive smooth texture. Master this stitch and you're ready to tackle any toy project!

1. Insert hook into the stitch or chain (7).

2. Yarn over and pull one loop through the stitch – two loops on the hook (8).

3. Yarn over and pull yarn through the two loops to complete the stitch (9).

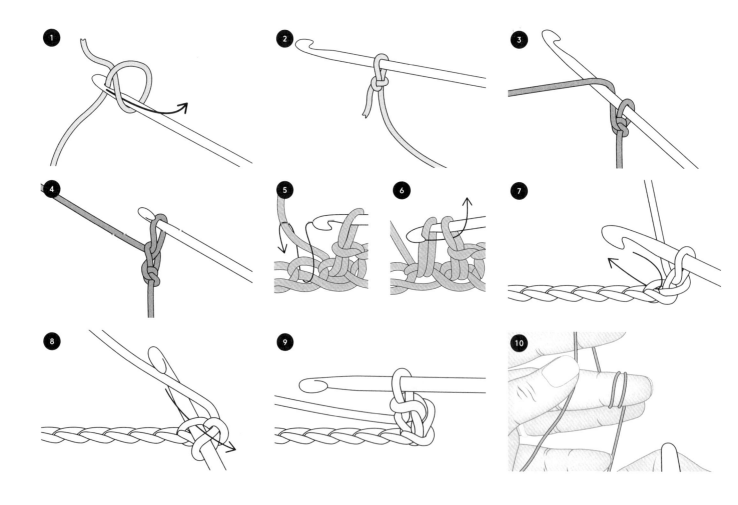

Magic ring

The magic ring method creates a secure beginning that's unlikely to unravel.

1. Take the yarn tail and wrap it twice around your middle finger **(10)**.

2. Insert hook under the wrapped yarn, yarn over and pull one loop through to the front **(11 and 12)**.

3. Yarn over again and pull the yarn through the loop on the hook – this loop doesn't count as a stitch.

4. Insert hook under the wrapped yarn, yarn over and pull one loop through to the front **(13)**.

5. Yarn over and pull the yarn through the two loops on the hook – this counts as the first single crochet stitch.

6. Repeat steps 4 and 5 the number of times needed. Then pull the two strands and the yarn tail to tighten the ring **(14 and 15)**.

Right side/wrong side

For amigurumi pieces worked in the round, it's easy to tell the right side of the work from the wrong side. The right side has a smooth texture, with each stitch forming a little 'v' **(16)**. The wrong side has dashes running along each round **(17)**.

Front Loops/back Loops

If you look closely at the top edge of your crochet, you will see the two loops that make up the top of each stitch. When working most stitches, the hook is inserted under both loops; however, sometimes it's useful to work in only the front loop or the back loop. When working in the round, the front loop is always the loop closest to the right side of the fabric. The back loop is the one closest to the wrong side of the fabric.

Working into the back bar (hump/third loop) of a chain

The front of the foundation chain appears as a series of 'v's **(18)**. Turn over the foundation chain and you will see a row of bumps along the top. These bumps are often called back humps, back bars or third loops. Working into the back bars gives a neat working edge to both sides of the chain **(19)**.

Single crochet increase (inc)

Strategically placed increases are used to grow and to shape the toys. An increase is simply two or more single crochet stitches worked into the same starting stitch.

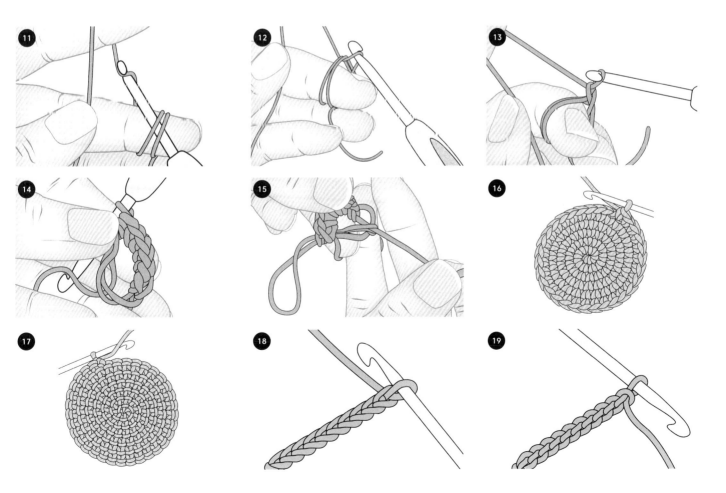

single crochet decrease (dec)

1. Insert the hook into the first stitch, yarn over and pull one loop through the stitch (two loops on hook).

2. Insert the hook into the second stitch, yarn over and pull one loop through the stitch (three loops on hook).

3. Yarn over and pull one loop through all loops on the hook.

invisible single crochet decrease (inv dec)

An invisible decrease helps to maintain the smooth texture of the finished amigurumi; when worked correctly it is nearly impossible to tell apart from a regular single crochet.

1. Insert the hook under the front loop of the first stitch and through both loops of the next stitch (20).

2. Yarn over and pull one loop through all loops from the two stitches (21).

3. Yarn over and pull one loop through the two loops on hook to complete (22).

single crochet 3 together (sc3tog)

1. Insert the hook into the first stitch, yarn over and pull one loop through the stitch (two loops on hook).

2. Insert the hook into the second stitch, yarn over and pull one loop through the stitch (three loops on hook).

3. Insert the hook into the third stitch, yarn over and pull one loop through the stitch (four loops on hook).

4. Yarn over and pull one loop through all loops on the hook.

invisible single crochet 3 together (inv sc3tog)

1. Insert the hook under the front loop of the first and second stitch and through both loops of the third stitch (23).

2. Yarn over and pull one loop through all loops from the three stitches (two loops on hook) (24).

3. Yarn over and pull one loop through two loops on the hook to complete (25).

Half double crochet (hdc)

Half double crochet is a little taller than single crochet and has an extra yarn over in it to add height.

1. Yarn over, insert the hook into the stitch or chain (26).

2. Yarn over and pull one loop through the stitch – three loops on the hook. Yarn over and pull one loop through all loops on the hook to complete the stitch (27).

Half double crochet 2 together (hdc2tog)

1. Yarn over, insert the hook into the first stitch, yarn over and pull one loop through the stitch (three loops on hook).

2. Yarn over, insert the hook into the second stitch, yarn over and pull one loop through the stitch (five loops on hook).

3. Yarn over and pull one loop through all five loops on the hook.

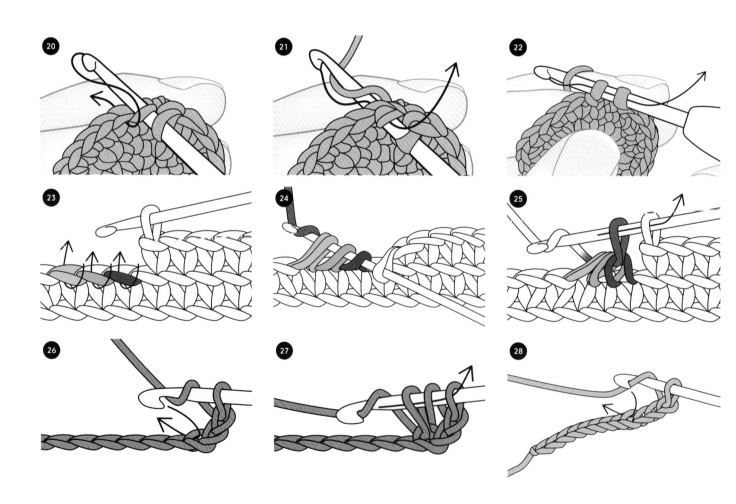

Double crochet (dc)

1. Yarn over, insert hook into the stitch or chain **(28)**.

2. Yarn over, pull one loop through the stitch – three loops on the hook **(29)**.

3. Yarn over, pull one loop through the first two loops – two loops on hook **(30)**.

4. Yarn over, pull one loop through both loops on hook to complete the stitch **(31)**.

Treble crochet (tr)

The tallest stitch – very useful for spikes and feather details.

1. Yarn over twice so there are two wraps on hook, insert the hook into the stitch or chain **(32)**.

2. Yarn over, pull one loop through the stitch – four loops on hook.

3. Yarn over, pull one loop through the first two loops – three loops on hook **(33)**.

4. Yarn over, pull one loop through the next two loops – two loops on hook.

5. Yarn over, pull one loop through both loops on the hook to complete the stitch.

Crab stitch

This stitch is also called reverse single crochet. It can be a bit tricky to get the hang of at first, so be patient with the stitches!

1. Insert the hook into the stitch just worked, reversing the direction of the round **(34)**.

2. Yarn over, pull one loop through – two loops on the hook **(35)**.

3. Yarn over, pull one loop through both loops on hook to complete the stitch. Carry on working in the reverse direction – notice how the stitches are now creating a twisty bumpy edge along the top **(36)**.

Changing colours

For a neat colour change, introduce the new colour on the last loop of the previous stitch. This way the correct colour loop will sit over the next stitch **(37)**.

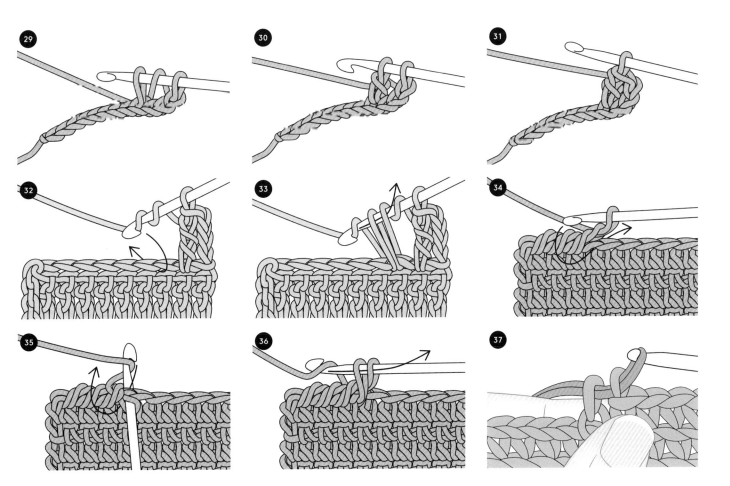

ASSEMBLY TECHNIQUES

sewing

Many of the appendages in this book are assembled by joining in with crochet, for example, a tail might pick up where the body ends; however, a bit of sewing will also come in handy. Pinning the pieces in place before you start will help to ensure everything is positioned in the best spot. **(photo 1)**

To blend an added piece in with the rest of the fabric, try putting the needle under the front posts of the stitches rather than the top two working loops. **(photo 2)**

For a shape that needs to have a defined, raised edge try a back stitch under the top loops. Take your time when attaching the pieces, stitching through each crochet stitch, and if something doesn't look quite right, either keep it as a natural quirk or unpick and try again! **(photo 3)**

stuffing

When stuffing the toys take care to fill them out evenly and check how squishy the toy feels. The filling shouldn't feel too tight and stiff; it should bounce back into shape when pressed. Roll the finished shape between your hands to spread the filling evenly.

To add an extra tactile element to the finished toy, you could add some plastic beads or cherry stones in a secure pouch into the tummy or feet. For some of my projects in the past I've added rattle inserts and squeakers – great for gifting to little ones.

closing the piece

To mimic the magic ring beginning, use a tapestry needle to sew up at the end.

1. Pick up all the front loops of the last round with a tapestry needle. **(photo 4)**

2. Pull tight to close and hide the yarn tail inside the work. **(photos 5 and 6)**

ABOUT THE AUTHOR

Irene Strange is a pen name for Irina Palczynski, a crochet designer and amigurumi maker living near London, UK. Learning to crochet and knit as a child, Irina began her current crochet adventure back in 2008, starting with small presents for friends and family. Not surprisingly, she hasn't stopped making crochet creatures since! As well as independently releasing stand-alone designs, Irina is a frequent contributor to *Inside Crochet* and *Mollie Makes* magazines, the *Zoomigurumi* books series, and, together with Ilaria Caliri of Airali Design, the co-author of the 'Amigurumi Adventures' crochet-along seasonal events. Her other interests include tea drinking, growing wonky shaped veg at the allotment and exploring the great outdoors with the family.

www.irenestrange.co.uk

Instagram.com/irenestrange

ACKNOWLEDGMENTS

While designing new crochet characters can be a solitary task, it truly takes a village to turn those designs into a book.

I would like to thank my husband Ben, for his constant support and the many cups of tea brewed while I was making this book. Also our children, Nicky and Lizzy, for greeting each new creature with tons of enthusiasm and for thoroughly hug-testing every sample.

To my grandma Larissa, for introducing me to the world of crafts and encouraging me always, even when we were living 1,550 miles apart.

To my mother Svetlana, for indulging my crafty exploits since my teenage years, and my dad Richard, without whose last name there probably wouldn't be an Irene Strange.

A big thank you to Ame Verso, Jeni Chown and Lindsay Kaubi and the lovely team at David and Charles for helping me to focus on the creative process and navigate the curious world of book publishing – it has truly been a pleasure to work with all of you!

And, of course, a special thank you to you, the readers of this book – I can't wait to share this crochet adventure with you!

index

A DAVID AND CHARLES BOOK
© David and Charles, Ltd 2022

David and Charles is an imprint of David and Charles, Ltd
Suite A, Tourism House, Pynes Hill, Exeter, EX2 5WS

Text and Designs © Irina Palczynski 2022
Layout and Photography © David and Charles, Ltd 2022

First published in the UK and USA in 2022

Irina Palczynski has asserted her right to be identified as author of this work in accordance with the Copyright, Designs and Patents Act, 1988.

A catalogue record for this book is available from the British Library.

ISBN-13: 9781446309018 paperback
ISBN-13: 9781446381328 EPUB
ISBN-13: 9781446381311 PDF

This book has been printed on paper from approved suppliers and made from pulp from sustainable sources.

Printed in the UK by Buxton Press for:
David and Charles, Ltd
Suite A, Tourism House, Pynes Hill, Exeter, EX2 5WS

10 9 8 7 6 5 4 3 2 1

Publishing Director: Ame Verso
Managing Editor: Jeni Chown
Project Editor: Lindsay Kaubi
Designer: Sam Staddon
Illustrations: Kuo Kang Chen & Ethan Danielson
Art Direction: Prudence Rogers
Photography: Jason Jenkins, Chris Grady & Irene Strange
Production Manager: Beverley Richardson

David and Charles publishes high-quality books on a wide range of subjects. For more information visit www.davidandcharles.com.

Share your makes with us on social media using #dandcbooks and follow us on Facebook and Instagram by searching for @dandcbooks.

Layout of the digital edition of this book may vary depending on reader hardware and display settings.